InSight™

A MEDIA LAB IN EXPERIMENTAL PSYCHOLOGY

John Baro
Wheeling Jesuit University

THOMSON

BROOKS/COLE

Australia • Canada • Mexico • Singapore • Spain • United Kingdom • United States

Printed in Canada
1 2 3 4 5 6 7   07 06 05 04 03

Printer: Webcom

ISBN: 0-534-64036-2

For more information about our products, contact us at:
Thomson Learning Academic Resource Center
1-800-423-0563

For permission to use material from this text, contact us by:
Phone: 1-800-730-2214
Fax: 1-800-731-2215
Web: http://www.thomsonrights.com

Brooks/Cole—Thomson Learning
10 Davis Drive
Belmont, CA 94002-3098
USA

Asia
Thomson Learning
5 Shenton Way #01-01
UIC Building
Singapore 068808

Australia/New Zealand
Thomson Learning
102 Dodds Street
Southbank, Victoria 3006
Australia

Canada
Nelson
1120 Birchmount Road
Toronto, Ontario M1K 5G4
Canada

Europe/Middle East/South Africa
Thomson Learning
High Holborn House
50/51 Bedford Row
London WC1R 4LR
United Kingdom

Latin America
Thomson Learning
Seneca, 53
Colonia Polanco
11560 Mexico D.F.
Mexico

Spain/Portugal
Paraninfo
Calle/Magallanes, 25
28015 Madrid, Spain

Original concept and
program content by
John A. Baro and
Stephen Lehmkuhle

Interface design and
programming by
John A. Baro
Graphic design by
Rhonda Sellers Baro

InSight™ Student Guide

Quick Start

RUNNING INSIGHT

No installation or setup is required to run *InSight*™—the program runs entirely from the CD.

Windows® Users: *InSight* should start automatically. If it doesn't, double click **My Computer** on your desktop. Right click the CD-ROM icon, then select **Open**. Double-click **InSight.exe**.

Macintosh® OS 8 or 9 Users: Open the CD-ROM on your desktop, then double-click the **InSight OS 9** icon.

Macintosh® OS X Users: Open the CD-ROM on your desktop, then double-click the **InSight OS X** icon.

DISPLAY SETTINGS

InSight requires your display to be set to millions of colors (24- or 32-bit color on Windows). To check your display setting:

Windows® Users: Right-click on the Windows **Desktop** to bring up the **Display Properties** window, then click the **Settings** tab.

Macintosh® OS 8 or 9 Users: Select the **Monitors** control panel (on some systems it may be called **Monitors & Sound**) from the **Apple** menu.

Macintosh® OS X Users: Select **System Preferences...** from the **Apple** menu, then under **Hardware** click **Displays**.

MINIMUM SYSTEM REQUIREMENTS

	Macintosh®	Windows®
Computer	PowerPC® 200 MHz (G3 or greater recommended)	Pentium® 233 MHz (500 MHz or above recommended)
Display	800 x 600 pixels millions of colors	800 x 600 pixels 24- or 32-bit color
CD Drive	8X	8X
Memory	64 MB RAM	64 MB RAM
Sound		16-bit sound card
System	Mac OS 8.6	Windows 98 (not NT)
Software	Adobe Acrobat Reader® 3.0	Adobe Acrobat Reader® 3.0

RECOMMENDED

- Speakers or headphones
- Printer
- 3D glasses are required for some modules.

  Visit the Wadsworth Web site for information on purchasing 3D glasses:

  http://www.wadsworth.com/psychology_d/templates/student_resources/0534640370/cdrom/weblinks/index.html

Scaling Vision

OBJECTIVES

By completing this exercise, you will learn:

- our perception of magnitude is not necessarily the same as the actual magnitude of objects.

- that the visual system uses different kinds of scales to measure the magnitude of different kinds of stimuli.

- about using a magnitude estimation procedure to create a scale of visual perception.

- about collecting, analyzing, interpreting, and presenting scientific data.

GETTING STARTED

Before beginning this exercise go to the **Scaling Vision** experiment and click the **Info** button. Read the **Background** information and **Instructions** for additional information you will need to complete the exercise.

INSTRUCTIONS

The following is a brief summary of the program instructions:

- Before beginning the experiment for the first time select **Practice** to become familiar with the experimental procedure.

- To begin a block of trials select **Experiment**.

- After you finish each block of trials you will be taken to the **Results** screen. After viewing your results select **Experiment** to begin another block of trials.

- On the **Results** screen click the **Data Suggestions** button for suggestions on how to interpret or present your data.

EXERCISE

You can complete this exercise in any of three ways:

- Answer each question listed below, one at a time as you go,
- use the questions as a guide to prepare a written research report, or
- use the questions as a guide to prepare an oral presentation.

From the **Main** screen go to **About Science: Research Report** for suggestions on preparing a report or presentation.

INTRODUCTION

After you have finished reading the **Background** information you should be familiar with what scales are, using a magnitude estimation procedure to create a scale, and the different types of visual scales. Before beginning an experiment it is important to understand the question(s) you are trying to answer and what the most likely answers are.

In this experiment you will be investigating how general visual scales are. In other words, does the visual system use a different kind of scale for different stimuli, or does the visual system use a similar scale for many different kinds of stimuli? You will be comparing two different kinds of stimuli—**Brightness** (brightness of a spot) and **Dots** ("whiteness" of a random-dot pattern)—and the way the visual system scales each.

Before you begin a trial block, set the following experimental parameters:

Stimulus Range: Long

Stimulus Spacing: Linear

Standard Position: Middle

Standard Value: 100

You will be running two blocks of trials, one for each of the two different stimuli. Linear spacing means that there is the same distance between each of the stimuli. For example, if you were estimating line length, the test stimuli might be 10, 20, 30, 40 and 50 cm. In this example, a middle standard would mean that the standard stimulus is 30 cm. A high standard might be 50 cm.

The **Background** information discusses the different types of scales that the visual system might potentially use. In this experiment the stimuli will be spaced linearly—that means that there is an equal amount of distance between the magnitude of each of the test stimuli. If the visual system scales these stimuli according to their actual magnitudes you would expect to create a linear scale with this procedure. If your perception of the magnitudes of the stimuli is not the same as their actual magnitudes you would expect to create a log or a power function scale.

✍ State briefly, and in your own words, what question(s) you will be investigating, how you will do the experiment, and what you expect to find in your experiment.

COLLECTING DATA

To complete your data collection you must complete two blocks of 40 trials each. The parameter settings will be the same for each trial block, but the stimulus will be different. You will select two of the three available stimuli, **Dots** and **Brightness**—one in each trial block. Be sure to read the instructions carefully so that you understand what you will be estimating for each of the different types of stimulus.

✍ Describe the experimental procedure that you used. Be sure to include a description of the stimuli and how you responded to the stimuli. The general rule is to describe the procedure in enough detail so that someone who is unfamiliar with the procedure could do the exact same experiment just from reading your description.

ANALYZING YOUR DATA

When you have finished data collection the program will present a summary of your results. This summary includes three graphs for each condition. These graphs plot your estimates (on the vertical axes) versus the actual stimulus magnitudes (on the horizontal axes) on linear, semi-log, and log scales. The data are the same in each plot, only the way the graph axes are scaled is different. Also shown in the lower-right corner of each graph is the correlation coefficient, r^2. If all points in the plot fell exactly along a straight line this value would be 1.00. If these points were arranged randomly this value would be 0.00. The closer these values are to 1.00, the straighter the line. *(If any of these values is negative, or less than zero, it means that the line is upside down—review the instructions to make sure you were estimating the magnitude of the stimuli correctly.)* Click on the **Data Suggestions** button for more information about interpreting your results.

✍ Prepare three graphs for each stimulus condition—plot the data for each condition on linear, semi-log and log graphs (or print the **Results** screen). You can use the raw data to calculate the means if you need the values to make your own graphs. Remember, the *correlation coeffiient* (the statistic displayed in the lower-right of each graph) tells you how straight the functions are.

INTERPRETING YOUR DATA

The final step is to make sense out of your results. The numbers and graphs by themselves don't mean anything until you interpret them.

Explain your results. Are your data best described by a linear, a semi-log, or a power (log-log) function? Did the two different stimuli produce similar results?

✍   Based on your data, what type of scale would you say the visual system uses for each of the stimuli? Is it the same type of scale for each stimulus you measured? Would your conclusions be the same if you based them on all the students in your class, rather than the results of just one observer?

✍   How would you go about creating a set of stimuli (for each of those you measured in the experiment) that *appeared* to all be spaced equally from one another? How would you space them so that an observer would judge the difference to be the same for both large and small stimuli?

✍   Good research often generates as many new questions as it answers. Are there any other questions that you could answer with this procedure or that this procedure left unanswered?

ADDITIONAL INVESTIGATIONS

* Compare the scale for the **Lines** stimulus to the **Brightness** and **Dots** scales. Does the visusl system use the same type of scale for each of these stimuli?

* Pick one of the stimuli and compare the results of the three **Stimulus Range** settings, **Short**, **Medium**, and **Long**. It has been observed for some stimuli that the scale can change at the high and/or low end of the stimulus range. Does your scale change with stimulus range?

* Pick one of the stimuli and compare the results of the two **Stimulus Spacing** settings, **Linear** and **Log**. If the stimuli are not spaced evenly (log spacing) does that affect the kind of scale you use?

* Pick one of the stimuli and compare the results of the three **Standard Position** settings, **Low**, **Middle**, and **High**. If the standard is high or low compared to the test stimuli, does that cause your scale to expand or contract?

* Compare the effects of **Stimulus Range**, **Stimulus Spacing**, or **Standard Position** on scales for all three stimuli.

Measuring Illusions

OBJECTIVES

By completing this exercise, you will learn:

- that illusions, just like most other perceptions, can be objectively measured.

- by measuring an illusion, we can find out what part(s) of an image are responsible for "causing" the illusion.

- the definition of point of subjective equality (PSE).

- how vision scientists can measure our perceptions using Yes-No and method of limits psychophysical procedures.

- collecting, analyzing, interpreting, and presenting scientific data.

GETTING STARTED

Before beginning this exercise go to the **Measuring Illusions** experiment and click the **Info** button. Read the **Background** information and **Instructions** for additional information you will need to complete the exercise.

INSTRUCTIONS

The following is a brief summary of the program instructions:

- Before beginning the experiment for the first time select **Practice** to become familiar with the experimental procedure.

- To begin a block of trials select **Experiment**.

- After you finish each block of trials you will be taken the to the **Results** screen. After viewing your results select **Experiment** to begin another block of trials.

- On the **Results** screen click the **Data Suggestions** button for suggestions on how to interpret or present your data.

EXERCISE

You can complete this exercise in any of three ways:

- Answer each question listed below, one at a time as you go,
- use the questions as a guide to prepare a written research report, or
- use the questions as a guide to prepare an oral presentation.

From the **Main** screen go to **About Science: Research Report** for suggestions on preparing a report or presentation.

INTRODUCTION

After you have finished reading the **Background** information you should be familiar with some kinds of visual illusions and why vision scientists study them. You should also understand how the Yes-No and method of limits procedures work. Before beginning an experiment it is important to understand the question(s) you are trying to answer and what the most likely answers are.

In this investigation you will be measuring the size of the Müller-Lyer illusion. (Look at the **Illusions and Aftereffect**s module if you would like to learn more about the Müller-Lyer illusion.) The measure of interest in this procedure is the *point of subjective equality*, or PSE. This will tell you how different the lines have to be for them to appear the same length. You will be measuring the PSE for three different experimental conditions—with **Short**, **Medium**, and **Long** arrowheads. When you compare these three PSEs you will be able to tell how the length of the arrowheads affects the size of the illusion (or if there is any effect at all).

✍ State briefly, and in your own words, what question(s) you will be investigating, how you will do the experiment, and what you expect to find in your experiment. Since you have no way of knowing what to expect in this experiment, make a reasonable guess as to how you think the length of the arrowheads will affect the size of this illusion (and be prepared to defend your guess *before you complete the experiment*).

COLLECTING DATA

To complete your data collection you must complete three blocks of trials, one for each of the stimulus conditions—**Short**, **Medium**, and **Long** arrowheads. Before beginning each trial block, select **Müller-Lyer Illusion** and set the **Arrowhead Length**. It doesn't matter in what order you complete the three conditions, unless you will be summarizing the results for several observers—then you should try to have different observers complete the conditions in different orders (that way you'll know if the order had an effect).

 Describe the experimental procedure that you used. Be sure to include a description of the stimuli and how you responded to the stimuli. The general rule is to describe the procedure in enough detail so that someone who is unfamiliar with the procedure could do the exact same experiment just from reading your description.

ANALYZING YOUR DATA

When you have finished data collection the program will present a summary of your results. You will be shown the two stimuli drawn at the PSE (in other words, they should appear equal). You will also be shown the actual numbers that correspond to the standard and test stimuli. In this case it is the length of the lines, in pixels.

Prepare a graph to compare the results of the three conditions. Remember, you are trying to show how the length of the arrowheads affects the size of the illusion, so that should be clear to someone looking at your graph.

INTERPRETING YOUR DATA

The final step is to make sense out of your results. The numbers and graphs by themselves don't mean anything until you interpret them.

Explain your results. Did you find an effect of arrowhead length on the size of the illusion? How could you explain the effect you observed? Did the experiment turn out the way you expected? If it didn't, why do you think it turned out the way it did?

Good research often generates as many new questions as it answers. Are there any other questions that you could answer with this procedure? Take a look at the **Illusions** and **Aftereffects** demonstration and see if there are any other illusions to which the results of this experiment might apply.

ADDITIONAL INVESTIGATIONS

- Compare the effects of the two **Vertical Line Position** settings—**From Top** and **From Bottom**—on the size of the **Horizontal-Vertical Illusion**. Give an explanation for your results.
- Compare the effects of three **Spot Size** settings—**Small**, **Medium**, and **Large**—on the size of the **Simultaneous Contrast** effect. Give an explanation for your results.

Global Precedence

OBJECTIVES

By completing this exercise, you will learn about:

- the anatomy of the visual system and how information gets from the eyes to the brain.

- how vision scientists can measure our perceptions— psychophysical methods.

- using a simple reaction time procedure to measure the speed at which the brain processes visual information.

- collecting, analyzing, interpreting, and presenting scientific data.

GETTING STARTED

Before beginning this exercise go to the **Global Precedence** experiment and click the **Info** button. Read the **Background** information and **Instructions** for additional information you will need to complete the exercise.

INSTRUCTIONS

The following is a brief summary of the program instructions:

- Before beginning the experiment for the first time select **Practice** to become familiar with the experimental procedure.

- To complete a block of trials select **Experiment** then select either **Respond to GLOBAL letters** or **Respond to LOCAL letters**, depending on which condition you would like to do.

- After you finish each block of trials you will be taken to the **Results** screen. After completing your first trial block select **Experiment** to begin the second block of trials.

- On the **Results** screen click the **Data Suggestions** button for suggestions on how to present your data.

EXERCISE

You can complete this exercise in any of three ways:

- Answer each question listed below, one at a time as you go,

- use the questions as a guide to prepare a written research report, or

- use the questions as a guide to prepare an oral presentation.

From the **Main** screen go to **About Science: Research Report** for suggestions on preparing a report or presentation.

INTRODUCTION

After you have finished reading the **Background** information you should be familiar with the way information is transmitted through the visual system and the way in which a reaction time procedure can be used to measure the speed of this process. Before beginning an experiment it is important to understand the question(s) you are trying to answer and what the most likely answers are.

 State briefly, and in your own words, what question(s) you will be investigating, how you will do the experiment, and what you expect to find in your experiment.

COLLECTING DATA

To complete your data collection you must complete two blocks of 40 trials each in both the **Global** and **Local** conditions. Viewing distance should be about 60 cm (24 in). *Sitting at the correct viewing distance is especially important in this experiment.* It doesn't matter in what order you complete the two conditions, unless you will be summarizing the results for several observers—then you should try to have different observers complete the conditions in different orders (that way you'll know if the order had an effect).

Describe the experimental procedure that you used. Be sure to include a description of the stimuli and how you responded to the stimuli. The general rule is to describe the procedure in enough detail so that someone who is unfamiliar with the procedure could do the exact same experiment just from reading your description.

ANALYZING YOUR DATA

When you have finished data collection the program will present a summary of your results. This summary includes for each condition the number of correct responses, mean reaction times (averages), and standard errors. (From the **Main** screen go to **About Science: Data Analysis** to learn about standard errors.)

 Prepare a graph that shows the difference in reaction times to global and local stimuli. You will need to combine the data across different conditions for this graph. Calculate two means—one for the four global conditions and one for the four local conditions.

INTERPRETING YOUR DATA

The final step is to make sense out of your results. The numbers and graphs by themselves don't mean anything until you interpret them.

 Explain your results. Did you find any differences between the global and local conditions? Was the outcome what you expected? If it wasn't, why do you think it turned out the way it did?

Good research often generates as many new questions as it answers. Are there any other questions that you could answer with this procedure.

ADDITIONAL INVESTIGATIONS

- Compare the *consistent* (global and local letters the same) versus the *inconsistent* (global and local letters different) trials.

- Look at the number of incorrect responses. Were there more/less for global versus local trials? Were there more/less for consistent versus inconsistent trials?

Feature Analysis

OBJECTIVES

By completing this exercise, you will learn:

- that our visual system breaks down complex textures into simple building blocks before analyzing them.
- that our visual system uses two different methods to analyze textures, serial and parallel.
- about using a choice reaction-time procedure to measure the speed at which the brain processes visual information.
- collecting, analyzing, interpreting, and presenting scientific data.

GETTING STARTED

Before beginning this exercise go to the **Feature Analysis** experiment and click the **Info** button. Read the **Background** information and **Instructions** for additional information you will need to complete the exercise.

INSTRUCTIONS

The following is a brief summary of the program instructions:

- Before beginning the experiment for the first time select **Practice** to become familiar with the experimental procedure.
- Before beginning a block of trials select a **Target/Distractor** stimulus combination.
- To begin a block of trials select **Experiment**. A sample of the target (the stimulus you will be looking for) will be shown at the bottom of the screen.
- After you finish each block of trials you will be taken the to the **Results** screen. After viewing your results select **Experiment** to begin another block of trials.
- On the **Results** screen click the **Data Suggestions** button for suggestions on how to interpret or present your data.

EXERCISE

You can complete this exercise in any of three ways:

- Answer each question listed below, one at a time as you go,
- use the questions as a guide to prepare a written research report, or
- use the questions as a guide to prepare an oral presentation.

From the **Main** screen go to **About Science: Research Report** for suggestions on preparing a report or presentation.

INTRODUCTION

After you have finished reading the **Background** information you should be familiar with the ways the visual system analyzes features, and the way in which a reaction time procedure can be used to measure the speed of this process. Before beginning an experiment it is important to understand the question(s) you are trying to answer and what the most likely answers are.

In this investigation you will be trying to determine whether the visual system uses a parallel or a serial process to analyze different types of features. Remember, with parallel processing you can "look at" all the items in a stimulus display at once, so it shouldn't matter how many distractor items are present. But with serial processing you need to do a visual search and processing should be slower when there are more distractors.

You will be comparing two sets of stimuli to determine how they are processed by the visual system. One set consists of green targets (**Green/Not Green**—the target is any item that is green), and parallel lines with end lines (**Same Ends/Different Ends**—see the table below). In the second set you will be comparing the same stimuli using each one as the target and distractor (**Line-Circles/No Line-Circles** and **No Line-Circles/Line-Circles**—see the table below). You will be completing a total of four trial blocks. *When selecting stimuli the first item is the target and the second item is the distractor.*

State briefly, and in your own words, what question(s) you will be investigating, how you will do the experiment, and what you expect to find in your experiment. Based on the **Background** information make a prediction about which of the targets will be processed pre-attentively (in parallel) and which will be processed attentively (serially).

COLLECTING DATA

To complete your data collection you must complete 4 blocks of 36 trials each. The stimulus conditions are:

Target/Distractor

 Green/Not Green

Same Ends/Different Ends

Line-Circles/No Line–Circles

No Line–Circles/Line–Circles

Be sure to complete a block of practice trials before you begin and *be sure to run the stimulus (target/distractor) conditions shown above.*

When your data are analyzed only trials on which you made a correct response are counted, so if you make a large number of incorrect responses run the trial block over again. It doesn't matter in what order you complete the three conditions unless you will be summarizing the results for several observers—then you should try to have different observers complete the conditions in different orders (that way you'll know if the order had an effect).

 Describe the experimental procedure that you used. Be sure to include a description of the stimuli and how you responded to the stimuli. The general rule is to describe the procedure in enough detail so that someone who is unfamiliar with the procedure could do the exact same experiment just from reading your description.

ANALYZING YOUR DATA

When you have finished data collection the program will present a summary of your results. This summary includes for each condition, mean reaction times (averages) for 2, 8, and 32 distractor items. When you view your results, be sure you are looking at the **Plot All Trials** screen (instead of the **Plot Present vs. Absent** screen).

 Prepare two graphs—one to compare the **Green/Not Green** and **Same Ends/Different Ends** conditions, and another to compare the **Line-Circles/No Line-Circles** and **No Line-Circles/Line-Circles** conditions. Depending on the order you complete the different conditions, you may need to save your results and open them again to create a graph with only two conditions plotted.

INTERPRETING YOUR DATA

The final step is to make sense out of your results. The numbers and graphs by themselves don't mean anything until you interpret them.

✍ Explain your results. Were there any differences in RTs between the two pairs of stimuli? Which of the stimuli are processed pre-attentively (in parallel) and which are processed attentively (serially)? Was the outcome what you expected? If it wasn't, why do you think it turned out the way it did?

✍ Good research often generates as many new questions as it answers. Are there any other questions that you could answer with this procedure? Based on your results, could you make predictions about any of the other stimuli available in the experiment? For example, what do you think would happen if you reversed the roles of target and distractor in the **Green/Not Green** or in the **Same Ends/Different Ends** conditions?

ADDITIONAL INVESTIGATIONS

- There are many other target/distractor stimuli available. Pick one (or more) of the other stimuli and predict—*before you collect any data*—whether the stimuli will be processed pre-attentively or attentively. Provide justification for your prediction (you can base it on your previous results). Do your experimental results support your prediction(s)? Do your predictions improve after you collect data for more stimuli?

- After you have collected data for several different stimuli create a set of rules that you could use to predict the results for new stimuli. In other words, what generalizations could you make about the characteristics of stimuli that are processed pre-attentively versus those that are processed attentively?

- Try to come up with an explanation for why switching some target/ distractor pairs can produce completely different results. In other words, why do you think switching a stimulus from target to distractor, or vice versa, would change the way your brain processes the information.

Depth Perception

OBJECTIVES

By completing this exercise, you will learn:

- how the visual system uses the 2D (flat) images seen by the two eyes to construct a 3D image of the world.

- the limits of our visual system in regard to seeing depth.

- how vision scientists can measure our perceptions—psychophysical methods.

- about using a magnitude estimation procedure to measure the size of a perception, in this case depth.

- about collecting, analyzing, interpreting, and presenting scientific data.

GETTING STARTED

Before beginning this exercise go to the **Depth Perception** experiment and click the **Info** button. Read the **Background** information and **Instructions** for additional information you will need to complete the exercise.

INSTRUCTIONS

The following is a brief summary of the program instructions:

- Before beginning the experiment for the first time select **Practice** to become familiar with the experimental procedure.

- To complete a block of trials select **Experiment**, and select either the **Crossed** or **Uncrossed Disparity** condition.

- Wear the red/green (or red/blue) glasses when viewing the stimuli. The *red* lens goes over your *right* eye. *It is important that you do not reverse the glasses for this experiment, or the disparities will be reversed.*

- After you finish each block of trials you will be taken the to the **Results** screen. After completing your first trial block select **Experiment** to begin the second block.

- On the **Results** screen click the **Data Suggestions** button for suggestions on how to present your data.

EXERCISE

You can complete this exercise in any of three ways:

- Answer each question listed below, one at a time as you go,

- use the questions as a guide to prepare a written research report, or

- use the questions as a guide to prepare an oral presentation.

From the **Main** screen go to **About Science: Research Report** for suggestions on preparing a report or presentation.

INTRODUCTION

After you have finished reading the **Background** information you should be familiar with the way in which the visual system creates our perception of a three-dimensional (3D) world. You should also be familiar with the terms **disparity**, **diplopia**, and **Panum's fusional area**. For a review of these terms and other concepts go to the **Depth Perception** experiment and click the **Info** button. Before beginning an experiment it is important to understand the question(s) you are trying to answer and what the most likely answers are.

In this experiment you will be measuring how the perception of depth changes with changes in the disparity of an image. You will also obtain a measure of the limits of depth perception (in other words, the size of Panum's fusional area). Beyond these limits the visual system cannot create a good perception of depth and you see double (diplopia). You will be comparing both crossed (in front) and uncrossed (behind) disparities—in some people, Panum's fusional area is asymmetrical (not the same size in both directions).

 State briefly, and in your own words, what question(s) you will be investigating, how you will do the experiment, and what you expect to find in your experiment.

COLLECTING DATA

Before beginning the experiment complete a block of practice trials. Some people do not see the depth in these stimuli immediately—you may need to view them for a few seconds before you see anything. View them from directly in front of the monitor.

To complete your data collection you must complete two blocks of 30 trials each in both the **Crossed** and **Uncrossed Disparity** conditions. Your viewing distance should be about 60 cm (24 in). *Sitting at the correct viewing distance is especially important in this experiment.* If you change your viewing distance during the experiment, the disparities of the binocular images will change.

It doesn't matter in what order you complete the two conditions, unless you will be summarizing the results for several observers—then you should try to have different observers complete the conditions in different orders (that way you'll know if the order had an effect).

✍ Describe the experimental procedure that you used. Be sure to include a description of the stimuli and how you responded to the stimuli. The general rule is to describe the procedure in enough detail so that someone who is unfamiliar with the procedure could do the exact same experiment just from reading your description.

ANALYZING YOUR DATA

When you have finished data collection the program will present a summary of your results. This summary includes a graph that plots your estimates of the perceived depth of the stimuli versus the actual disparity of the stimuli, for both the crossed and uncrossed disparity conditions. (The disparity, or difference between the left and right eyes' views, is measured in pixels—the tiny dots that make up the picture on the computer monitor.) The points at which you reported diplopia (seeing double) are also marked on the graph. The area between these points is an estimate of your Panum's fusional area. Click on the **Data Suggestions** button for a more detailed explanation of this graph.

If your data appear to be "backwards," as compared to the sample data (click the **Data Suggestions** button to see the sample data), it probably indicates that you were wearing the glasses backwards. If that happens you do not need to do the experiment over—just reverse your data. The crossed disparity condition would actually be uncrossed, and vice versa.

✍ Prepare a graph similar to the one presented by the program that shows both disparity conditions (or print the **Results** screen). Remember, you're trying to show (1) how your perception of depth changed with changes in disparity, and (2) the limits of Panum's fusion area.

INTERPRETING YOUR DATA

The final step is to make sense out of your results. The numbers and graphs by themselves don't mean anything until you interpret them.

✍ Explain your results. How did your perception of depth change with the disparity of the stimulus? In other words, did the stimuli appear to have more or less depth as disparity increased? What does that tell you about the way disparity information is used by the visual system to create a perception of depth? Was the outcome what you expected? If it wasn't, why do you think it turned out the way it did?

✍ What happened to your perception of depth beyond the limits of Panum's fusional area? Did the change in depth continue in the same direction, or did it reverse?

✍️   In some people, Panum's fusional area is asymmetrical—it is wider in one direction than the other (for crossed versus uncrossed disparity). Was your Panum's fusional area symmetrical or asymmetrical?

✍️   For some people, the stimuli in this experiment might not be beyond Panum's fusional area. These people would be able to fuse all the stimuli without ever seeing double. If this was true for you, what do you think that means?

✍️   Good research often generates as many new questions as it answers. Are there any new questions that the results of this experiment suggest to you?

ADDITIONAL INVESTIGATIONS

Change your viewing distance to 30 cm (12 in) (half the viewing distance), or 120 cm (48 in) (double the viewing distance). What happens to the disparity of the dots when you change the viewing distance? How would you expect your measure of Panum's fusional area to change? Does it change as expected?

Contrast Sensitivity—Method of Adjustment

OBJECTIVES

By completing this exercise, you will learn:

- the meaning of contrast, threshold, sensitivity, spatial frequency, and contrast sensitivity function.

- how sensitivity to contrast varies with spatial frequency.

- how vision scientists can measure our perceptions—psychophysical methods.

- about using a method of adjustment procedure to measure the contrast detection threshold.

- about collecting, analyzing, interpreting, and presenting scientific data.

Note: Both procedures in this exercise measure the same thing. It is recommended that the half the class do the method of adjustment procedure and the other half do the forced choice procedure, then compare the results of the two procedures.

GETTING STARTED

Before beginning this exercise go to the **Contrast Sensitivity** experiment and click the **Info** button. Read the **Background** information and **Instructions** for additional information you will need to complete the exercise.

INSTRUCTIONS

The following is a brief summary of the program instructions:

- Before beginning the experiment for the first time select **Practice** to become familiar with the experimental procedure.

- To complete a block of trials select **Experiment**, then select **Method of Adjustment**.

- After you finish a block of trials you will be taken the to the **Results** screen.

- On the **Results** screen click the **Data Suggestions** button for suggestions on how to present your data.

EXERCISE

You can complete this exercise in any of three ways:

- Answer each question listed below, one at a time as you go,
- use the questions as a guide to prepare a written research report, or
- use the questions as a guide to prepare an oral presentation.

From the **Main** screen go to **About Science: Research Report** for suggestions on preparing a report or presentation.

INTRODUCTION

After you have finished reading the **Background** information you should be familiar with the method of adjustment procedure and the contrast sensitivity function (CSF). Before beginning an experiment it is important to understand the question(s) you are trying to answer and what the most likely answers are.

✍ State briefly, and in your own words, what question(s) you will be investigating, how you will do the experiment, and what you expect to find in your experiment.

COLLECTING DATA

To complete your data collection you must complete one block of 20 trials. Viewing distance should be about 57 cm (22 in). *Sitting at the correct viewing distance is especially important in this experiment.* If you change the viewing distance, you change the spatial frequency of the stimuli.

✍ Describe the experimental procedure that you used. Be sure to include a description of the stimuli and how you responded to the stimuli. The general rule is to describe the procedure in enough detail so that someone who is unfamiliar with the procedure could do the exact same experiment just from reading your description.

ANALYZING YOUR DATA

When you have finished data collection the program will present a summary of your results. This summary includes a contrast sensitivity function.

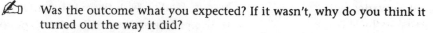 Prepare a graph that shows your contrast sensitivity function (or print the **Results** screen). In other words, plot your contrast sensitivity versus spatial frequency.

INTERPRETING YOUR DATA

The final step is to make sense out of your results. The numbers and graphs by themselves don't mean anything until you interpret them.

Explain your results. Did your contrast sensitivity vary with stimulus spatial frequency? If so, how?

Was the outcome what you expected? If it wasn't, why do you think it turned out the way it did?

What can you infer about vision in the "real world" from the results of this experiment?

Contrast Sensitivity—Forced Choice

OBJECTIVES

By completing this exercise, you will learn:

- the meaning of contrast, threshold, sensitivity, spatial frequency, and contrast sensitivity function.

- how sensitivity to contrast varies with spatial frequency.

- how vision scientists can measure our perceptions—psychophysical methods.

- about using a two-alternative forced choice procedure to measure the contrast detection threshold.

- about collecting, analyzing, interpreting, and presenting scientific data.

Note: Both procedures in this exercise measure the same thing. It is recommended that the half the class do the method of adjustment procedure and the other half do the forced choice procedure, then compare the results of the two procedures.

GETTING STARTED

Before beginning this exercise go to the **Contrast Sensitivity** experiment and click the **Info** button. Read the **Background** information and **Instructions** for additional information you will need to complete the exercise.

INSTRUCTIONS

The following is a brief summary of the program instructions:

- Before beginning the experiment for the first time select **Practice** to become familiar with the experimental procedure.

- To complete a block of trials select **Experiment**, then select **Forced Choice**. Before beginning a block of trials enter the experimental parameters.

- After you finish each block of trials you will be taken the to the **Results** screen. After viewing your results select **Experiment** to begin another block of trials.

- On the **Results** screen click the **Data Suggestions** button for suggestions on how to present your data.

EXERCISE

You can complete this exercise in any of three ways:

- Answer each question listed below, one at a time as you go,
- use the questions as a guide to prepare a written research report, or
- use the questions as a guide to prepare an oral presentation.

From the **Main** screen go to **About Science: Research Report** for suggestions on preparing a report or presentation.

INTRODUCTION

After you have finished reading the **Background** information you should be familiar with the forced choice procedure and the contrast sensitivity function (CSF). Before beginning an experiment it is important to understand the question(s) you are trying to answer and what the most likely answers are.

✍ State briefly, and in your own words, what question(s) you will be investigating, how you will do the experiment, and what you expect to find in your experiment.

COLLECTING DATA

To complete your data collection you must complete four trial blocks, one at each of the four spatial frequencies—1, 2, 4, and 8 c/deg. For each trial block enter:

Starting Contrast: 100

Stimulus Diameter: 100

Stimulus Duration: 64

Viewing distance should be about 57 cm (22 in). *Sitting at the correct viewing distance is especially important in this experiment.* If you change the viewing distance, you change the spatial frequency of the stimuli.

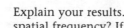 Describe the experimental procedure that you used. Be sure to include a description of the stimuli and how you responded to the stimuli. The general rule is to describe the procedure in enough detail so that someone who is unfamiliar with the procedure could do the exact same experiment just from reading your description.

ANALYZING YOUR DATA

When you have finished data collection the program will present a summary of your results. This summary includes a contrast sensitivity function.

Prepare a graph that shows your contrast sensitivity function (or print the **Results** screen). In other words, plot your contrast sensitivity versus spatial frequency.

INTERPRETING YOUR DATA

The final step is to make sense out of your results. The numbers and graphs by themselves don't mean anything until you interpret them.

Explain your results. Did your contrast sensitivity vary with stimulus spatial frequency? If so, how?

Was the outcome what you expected? If it wasn't, why do you think it turned out the way it did?

What can you infer about vision in the "real world" from the results of this experiment?

ADDITIONAL INVESTIGATIONS

- Compare three or more different **Stimulus Diameter** settings, for example 50, 100, and 200. Does stimulus size affect the overall sensitivity values or the shape of the contrast sensitivity function? Why do you think it should or shouldn't?

- Compare two or more different **Stimulus Duration** settings, for example 100 and 500. Does stimulus duration affect the overall sensitivity values or the shape of the contrast sensitivity function? Why do you think it should or shouldn't?

- Change your viewing distance to 28 cm (11 in) (half the viewing distance), or 114 cm (44 in) (double the viewing distance). What happens to the spatial frequency of the stimuli when you change the viewing distance? How would you expect the shape of the contrast sensitivity function to change? Does it change as expected?

Signal Detection

OBJECTIVES

By completing this exercise, you will learn:

- about signal detection theory and related concepts, including response criterion, signal and signal + noise distributions, and ROC curves.

- how vision scientists can measure our perceptions—psychophysical methods.

- about using two-alternative forced choice and rating-scale procedures.

- about collecting, analyzing, interpreting, and presenting scientific data.

GETTING STARTED

Before beginning this exercise go to the **Signal Detection** experiment and click the **Info** button. Read the **Background** information and **Instructions** for additional information you will need to complete the exercise.

INSTRUCTIONS

The following is a brief summary of the program instructions:

- Before beginning the experiment for the first time select **Practice** to become familiar with the experimental procedure.

- To complete a block of trials select **Experiment** and select a difficulty level.

- After you finish each block of trials you will be taken the to the **Results** screen. After completing your first trial block select **Experiment** to begin the second block of trials.

- On the **Results** screen click the **Data Suggestions** button for suggestions on how to present your data.

EXERCISE

You can complete this exercise in any of three ways:

- Answer each question listed below, one at a time as you go,

- use the questions as a guide to prepare a written research report, or

- use the questions as a guide to prepare an oral presentation.

From the **Main** screen go to **About Science: Research Report** for suggestions on preparing a report or presentation.

INTRODUCTION

After you have finished reading the **Background** information you should be familiar with the two-alternative forced choice procedure, rating scales, and the basics of signal detection theory. Before beginning an experiment, it is important to understand the question(s) you are trying to answer and what the most likely answers are.

In this experiment you will be measuring how well you can detect differences in small gaps in rings. Two large, black rings with small gaps in the top will be presented side by side. Your task is to determine which gap is larger. You will plot your results on ROC curves and compare your sensitivity to gaps of different sizes. In the **Difficult** condition the difference between the two gaps is very small (only one pixel); in the **Not So Easy** and **Easy** conditions the difference between the gaps is larger.

State briefly, and in your own words, what question(s) you will be investigating, how you will do the experiment, and what you expect to find in your experiment.

COLLECTING DATA

PLEASE NOTE: You must use each rating, 1–6, at least once in each trial block in order for an ROC curve to be calculated.

To complete your data collection you must complete three blocks of 72 trials each, one block of trials for each difficulty settings—**Easy**, **Not So Easy**, and **Difficult**. Viewing distance should be about 60 cm (24 in). It is important that you maintain the same viewing distance for all trials blocks. If you change your viewing distance during the experiment, you will not be able to compare results across trial blocks.

It doesn't matter in what order you complete the three conditions, unless you will be summarizing the results for several observers—then you should try to have different observers complete the conditions in different orders (that way you'll know if the order had an effect). Be sure to print or save your results after each trial block.

✍ Describe the experimental procedure that you used. Be sure to include a description of the stimuli and how you responded to the stimuli. The general rule is to describe the procedure in enough detail so that someone who is unfamiliar with the procedure could do the exact same experiment just from reading your description.

ANALYZING YOUR DATA

When you have finished data collection the program will present a summary of your results. This summary includes the number of times you used each rating and an ROC curve calculated from your ratings. Click on the **Data Suggestions** button for an explanation of how the ROC curve is calculated.

✍ Prepare three ROC curve graphs similar to the ones presented by the program (or print the **Results** screen). Be sure to include the area under the curve for each graph. Remember, you're trying to show how the area under the curves changes with gap size (difficulty level).

INTERPRETING YOUR DATA

The final step is to make sense out of your results. The numbers and graphs by themselves don't mean anything until you interpret them.

✍ Explain your results. Did the difference in gap sizes between the three conditions affect the area under the ROC curves? If so, how?

✍ Explain your results within the context of the underlying signal and signal + noise distributions. In other words, how would you infer that the width and/or spacing of the two distributions changed in the three conditions.

✍ Good research often generates as many new questions as it answers. Are there any new questions that the results of this experiment suggest to you?

ADDITIONAL INVESTIGATIONS

Change your viewing distance to 30 cm (12 in) (half the viewing distance), or 120 cm (48 in) (double the viewing distance). What happens to the size of the gap when you change the viewing distance? (Think about the gap size in terms of the size of its image on your retina.) How would you expect your ROC curve to change? Would the **Difficult** condition be more or less difficult when you move closer? Farther away? Does it change as expected?

Receptive Field Mapping

OBJECTIVES

By completing this exercise, you will learn about:

- the concept of visual receptive fields.

- how receptive fields differ in different parts of the visual system; how different types of cells respond to different types of stimuli.

- the technique used to identify and map receptive fields.

GETTING STARTED

Before beginning this exercise go to the **Receptive Field Mapping** demonstration and click the **Info** button. Read the **Background** information and **Instructions** for additional information you will need to complete the exercise.

INSTRUCTIONS

- Select a cell type—**Ganglion**, **LGN**, or **Cortex**.

- Select a stimulus—a **large spot**, a **small spot**, or one of several **bars** at different orientations.

- To *turn the stimulus off*, hold the mouse button down; to *turn the stimulus on*, release the mouse button.

- To *mark a receptive field*, press the space bar to turn the pencil on, then click the mouse where you want to make a mark. Press the space bar again to turn the pencil off.

- When you are satisfied that you have mapped both receptive fields on a screen click the **Show Fields** button. Once you show the receptive fields you can no longer continue to map them.

- For suggestions specific to a cell type click **Info** and look at the **Background** section.

EXERCISE

For this exercise, work in groups to map the receptive fields of four cells—two **Ganglion** *or* **LGN** cells, *and* two **Cortical** cells. There are two of each cell type on each screen. Each individual should do the mapping for at least one cell. If there are two students in your group, each should map two cells. If there are three students in your group, two students should map one cell, and one student should map two cells.

 Each student should print the screen showing the receptive fields they mapped.

Form and Motion

OBJECTIVES

By completing this exercise, you will learn about:

- how important motion is to the visual system.

- how we are capable of "seeing" depth and form where none exist, based on motion alone.

- how the visual system is especially sensitive to the motion of living things— "biological motion."

Note: On some computers, in particular some older Windows® laptops, you may see only the background dots and not the 3D shapes. If you have this problem, try one of the other 3D Renderer options—**Software** or **OpenGL**.

GETTING STARTED

Before beginning this exercise go to the **Form and Motion** demonstration and click the **Info** button. Read the **Background** information and **Instructions** for additional information you will need to complete the exercise.

INSTRUCTIONS

The following is a brief summary of the program instructions:

- Set **Object**, **Background**, and **Movie** parameters before making a random-dot movie.

- After you change one or more movie parameter settings you must make a movie before you can view it. To do this click the **Generate Movie** button.

- Click the **Play Movie** button to view an existing movie.

- Click the **Parameters** button to go back and change the settings.

- Click the **Reset** button to set all parameters to their original values.

EXERCISE

Number of Dots

Our visual system will try to create a perception of depth and form whenever possible. In fact, our visual system is so good at it that it needs very little information to create such a perception.

Click the **Reset** button to reset all movie settings to their original values. Select **Shape: Sphere** and **Background Type: None**. Click **Generate Movie** to make the movie. After the movie is finished *DO NOT* click the mouse to play the movie

 What did you see? In other words, what do the dots look like when they are *not* moving? Did you see any depth?

Now click the mouse to start the movie playing.

 What did you see? In other words, what do the dots look like when they are moving? Did you see any depth? Were the depth and form easy or difficult to see?

Go back to the **Parameters** screen and enter 50 for **Object: Number of Dots** (the first movie had 100 dots in the object). Click **Generate Movie** to make the movie, then click the mouse to play the movie.

 Did you still see the sphere? Was it more difficult to see?

Go back to the **Parameters** screen, generate and play movies with 25, 10, 5, 2, and 1 dot(s) in the object.

 Did you still see the sphere in each of these movies? Did it become more difficult to see with fewer and fewer dots? Could you see a sphere shape with only 1 or 2 dots? With only a few dots, do you think it would make a difference where on the sphere the dots are located? Try making new movies with only 1 or 2 dots (each time you make a new movie, the dots will be in different, random positions).

Please note: You need to change something to make a new movie, so switch between one and two dots.

 Do you think you would be able to see the other shapes (like the barbell, the paraboloid, or the cone) with less than ten dots in these objects?

The Effects of Noise

Noise is anything that interferes with what we are trying to see. Our visual system is usually very good at filtering out noise (most of what we see is noise).

Go to the **Parameters** screen and click the **Reset** button to reset the movie settings to their original values. Then select:

Shape: Sphere

Background Type: Stationary

Background Area: Overlaps Object

This will create a background pattern of dots that overlaps the sphere and does not move. Click **Generate Movie** to make the movie. After the movie is finished, *DO NOT* click the mouse to play the movie.

What did you see? In other words, what do the dots look like when they are not moving? Did you see any depth?

Now click the mouse to start the movie playing.

Could you see the sphere? Were the depth and form easy or difficult to see? Did the background interfere with your perception of the sphere?

Go to the **Parameters** screen and select **Background Type: Random** (the dots appear in random positions on each frame). Click **Generate Movie** to make the movie, then click the mouse to play the movie. Do the same with **Background Type: Random Motion** (the dots move in random directions) and **Background Type: Drifting** (the dots drift from right to left). For the Drifting background, select **Drift Speed: Medium**.

Which of the four backgrounds interfered most with your perception of the sphere? Which interfered least?

Try each of the four background types with 50 dots and then with 10 dots in the **Sphere**. **Select Object: Number of Dots** to set the number of dots in the object.

Could you see the sphere with 50 and 10 dots as easily as you could when there was no background? Which of the four backgrounds interfered most with your perception of the sphere with 50 dots? Did the same background interfere most when there were only 10 dots in the sphere?

Why do you think the backgrounds make it harder to see the object? Why do some backgrounds make it harder than others? To answer this, you need to think about what the visual system has to do to "create" a sphere from a bunch of moving dots—for each dot in each frame of the movie, the visual system needs to find a match in the next frame. Then it needs to figure out in what direction each dot is moving, which dots are moving together, and if the dots are moving together, do they appear to be part of a solid object. It's a pretty complicated process!

Biological Motion

Biological motion is the motion produced by living things. Our visual system is especially sensitive to biological motion.

Go to the **Parameters** screen and click the **Reset** button to reset the movie settings to their original values. Select **Shape: Biological** and **Backgrouond Type: None**. For the **Movie Frame Rate** enter 15. Click **Generate Movie** to make the movie. After the movie is finished *DO NOT* click the mouse to play the movie.

✍️ What did you see? In other words, what do the dots look like when they are not moving? Did you see any shape?

Now click the mouse to start the movie playing. You may need to adjust the movie frame rate, depending on how fast your computer is. Enter smaller frame rate values to slow down the movie or larger values to speed it up.

✍️ What did you see? What was the person doing? Is there anything you can tell about the person in the movie? For example, could you tell if it is a man or a woman?

Select **Rotation Axis: Upside Down**. Click **Generate Movie** to make the movie, then click the mouse to play the movie.

✍️ Does this make it harder to see what the person is doing? If so, why do you think that is? (Hint: Do you normally see people doing that particular activity upside down?)

Select **Rotation Axis: Normal** and select **Background Type: Random**. Click **Generate Movie** to make the movie, then click the mouse to play the movie.

✍️ Can you still see what the person is doing?

Select **Rotation Axis: Normal** and select **Background Type: Random Motion**. Click **Generate Movie** to make the movie, then click the mouse to play the movie. Do the same with **Background: Drifting**, **Drift Speed: Medium**.

✍️ Can you see what the person is doing with either of these backgrounds? Did adding a background have more or less of an effect on your perception of biological motion than it did on your perception of a rotating sphere? Why do you think that is?

Color & Motion

If you have completed the **Global Precedence** exercise you know that there are two pathways that carry information from the eyes to the brain. (For a review, go to the **Global Precedence** experiment, click **Info**, and read the **Background** information.) Each pathway carries different information, for example one carries information about large objects and the other carries information about small objects. Another difference between these pathways is that one can see color and the other can only see differences in brightness. Most researchers agree that the "color" pathway does not "see" motion very well—the "brightness" pathway is the "motion" pathway. Some researchers have reported that if you create a random-dot pattern where the dots and background are different colors but are the same brightness (so they can only be "seen" by the "color" pathway), that you cannot see the depth and form in the random-dot movies you made in this exercise. Other researchers however have not been able to replicate this finding.

See if you can create a movie in which the shape cannot be seen. Usually the colors used to make movies without brightness differences (i.e., luminance contrast) are red and green (for example, red dots on a green background).

Click the **Reset** button to reset all movie settings to their original values. Select **Shape: Sphere**. Set **Dots Color** and **Background Color** by clicking in the **colored boxes** and selecting a color from the popup color palette. Experiment with different combinations of shades of red and green.

(Hint: On most monitors, setting the green and red values the same will produce greens that are brighter than the reds.) The object is to make the red dots and the green background have the same luminance (brightness).

✎ Could you make a movie in which you could not see the shape?

Motion Aftereffect

There is a part of the visual system that is used for seeing motion. This part is divided up into several motion detectors and each of these detectors sees motion in only one direction. Motion detectors are arranged in pairs so that each member of a pair sees motion in the opposite direction (for example, one sees upward motion and the other sees downward motion). If we fatigue, or tire out, one member of a pair, then the other takes over temporarily.

For this part of the exercise go to the **Main** screen, then to the **Illusions and Aftereffects** demonstration. Click **Aftereffects** and select **Motion** from the popup menu. If you would like to see more information about this aftereffect click the **Help** button (it has a question mark on it) before you make your selection. The stimulus consists of two grating patterns. The grating on the top will drift to the left and the grating on the bottom will drift to the right for about a minute—these are the adapting stimuli. While the patterns are moving look at the white bar in the middle—*DO NOT* move your eyes or try to follow the moving patterns. When the movement stops, the test stimuli—two stationary gratings—will appear.

✎ Describe what happens to the test stimuli after the movement stopped. Were they still or did they appear to move? If they moved, did they move in the same direction or different directions? How was the motion of the aftereffect different from the motion of the adapting stimuli?

ADDITIONAL INVESTIGATIONS

- Repeat the **Number of Dots** manipulations (see above) on the other, non-biological shapes. Are any of the other shapes more or less affected by fewer dots than the sphere? Why?

- Repeat the **Effects of Noise** manipulations (see above) on the other, non-biological shapes. Are any of the other shapes more or less affected by noise than the sphere? Why?

- Try the various **Correlation** settings on the non-biological shapes. Try adding the different backgrounds. Explain how the correlation settings affect the moving dots. Can you still see the shape(s) at the lowest correlation? Can you still see the low-correlation shape(s) when a background is added? Why? Are you surprised by what you saw? Why?

Illusions and Aftereffects

OBJECTIVES

By completing this exercise, you will:

- see many different kinds of visual illusions.

- learn that sometimes by "fooling" our visual system, we can discover something about the way it works.

- see many different kinds of visual aftereffects.

- learn what visual aftereffects are and what they can tell us about how our visual system works.

Note: This exercise can be divided into two separate exercises. The first half of the exercise deals with illusions and the second half deals with aftereffects.

GETTING STARTED

Before beginning this exercise go to the **Illusions and Aftereffects** demonstration and click the **Info** button. Read the **Background** information and **Instructions** for additional information you will need to complete the exercise.

INSTRUCTIONS

The following is a brief summary of the program instructions:

- To view an *illusion* click **Motion, Depth, Contrast, Size, Shape, Orientation, Bistable,** or **Misc** and select an illusion from the popup menu.

- To view an *aftereffect* click the **Aftereffects** button and select one from the popup menu.

- For information about individual illusions or aftereffects click the **Help** button (it has a question mark on it). When help is turned on you will see information about each illusion before you view it. Reviewing this information may help you answer some of the questions below.

EXERCISE

Motion Illusions

Click **Motion** and select **Motion Reference** from the popup menu. You will see three dots moving back and forth. (Reviewing the information about each of these illusions may help you to answer some of the questions below.)

✍ How would you describe the path along which the middle dot is moving?

Click the **Hide Reference Dots** button to hide the top and bottom dots. If you want to show them again, click **Show Reference Dots.**

✍ Now how would you describe the path along which the middle dot is moving? Did your perception of the motion of the middle dot change when the top and bottom dots were not there.

Click **Motion** and select **Motion in Depth** from the popup menu. You will need to view this illusion with the red-green (or red/blue) glasses.

✍ Describe what you see. Now look at the display without the glasses and describe what you see. Why does the dot appear to be moving in depth?

If you have access to a television set and a pair of sunglasses (or any kind of dark filter or lens), try this: Set the television to a channel with no picture, so that all you see is static (that is, random black and white dots). Put the sunglass lens or dark filter over *one eye only* and view the static.

✍ Compare what the static looks like when viewed with and without the dark lens.

When viewing the static with the lens over one eye, you should see swirls of motion in depth. View the static first with the lens over your right eye, then with the lens over your left eye.

✍ Did the direction of the swirls of motion change when you switched eyes? When the lens was over your right eye, did you see mostly clockwise or counterclockwise motion (if it were viewed from the top)? How about when the lens was over you left eye?

Depth—Binocular Illusions

Click **Depth** and select **Binocular Suppression** from the popup menu. You will need to view this illusion with the red-green (or red/blue) glasses—put the red lens over your right eye. When you look at this illusions with the glasses, your right eye will see a horizontal line and your left eye will see two vertical lines. When each eye sees something completely different it confuses your visual system—this never happens in real life. So, your visual system tries to create a perception that is more realistic. Sometimes your perception will switch between what the left eye or the right eye sees, but at other times you will see a combination of both views. (Reviewing the information about each of these illusions may help you to answer some of the questions below.)

✍️ Describe what you see if you close your right eye or your left eye. Look at the image for a minute or two with both eyes. When the two images appear to be combined, what do you see (wearing the red-green glasses)?

Click **Depth** and select **Binocular Rivalry** from the popup menu. You will need to view this illusion with the red-green (or red/blue) glasses—put the red lens over your right eye. When you look at this illusions with the glasses, your right and left eyes will see two different images Sometimes you will perceive only one image or the other, but at other times you will see some combination of the two.

✍️ Look at the image for a minute or two with both eyes. Can you make yourself switch between the horizontal and vertical lines? When you only see one set of lines, what do you think happened to the other set? Do you sometimes see patches of vertical lines and patches of horizontal lines at the same time? Can you make yourself see both at the same place at the same time?

Size Illusions

Click **Size** and select **Müller-Lyer Illusion**, then **Ponzo Illusion**, then **Belboeuf Illusion** from the popup menu. Look at each of these illusions. (Reviewing the information about each of these illusions may help you to answer some of the questions below.)

✍️ Describe the illusions. Think of an explanation for each of these illusions. Why do you think they fool our visual system the way they do? Can the same explanation apply to all three? Be creative—there are no right or wrong answers because many illusions are not understood very well even by the "experts." The only requirement for a "good" answer here is that it makes sense.

Shape Illusions

Click **Shape** and select **Hering Illusion**, then **Converse Hering Illusion** from the popup menu. Look at each of these illusions.

✍️ Describe the illusions. Think of an explanation for these two illusions. Why do you think they fool our visual system the way they do? The same explanation should apply to both. As with those illusions above, there are no right or wrong answers.

Orientation (Tilt) Illusions

Click **Orientation** and select **Zöllner Illusion** from the popup menu.

✍️ Describe this illusion and think of an explanation for it. Why do you think it fools our visual system the way it does? Again, as long as your answer makes sense, it is "correct."

Click **Misc** and select **Illusory Contours** from the popup menu.

Describe what you see. Why do you think you see shapes where there are none?

Bistable Figures

Bistable figures aren't really illusions, but they are still fun to look at. They don't "fool" the visual system in the same way most illusions do—what they do is give the visual system two possible perceptions from which it must choose one. Look at each of the figures under the **Bistable Figures** popup menu.

Describe each of the two possible perceptions in each of the figures. Is it sometimes easier to see one than the other? Can you make yourself switch between each of the two perceptions whenever you like? Is it possible for you to see *both* perceptions *at the same time* in any of the figures?

Aftereffects

As the name implies, visual aftereffects are something you see *after* you look at something else. First you view an *adapting stimulus* for a minute or two, then you view a *test stimulus* that is similar to, but not exactly the same as, the adapting stimulus. After viewing the adapting stimulus, the test stimulus looks different than it normally would—that's the aftereffect. Most aftereffects last only a few seconds to a few minutes, but some can last hours or days. In some of these aftereffect demonstrations you will view the test stimulus both before and after you view the adapting stimulus, so you can compare how they look before and after you adapt.

Many aftereffects are caused by fatigue. One part of the visual system is "overworked" by the adapting stimulus and it becomes weakened. In the time before it recovers another part of the visual system works a little harder than normal. During the time that things are out of balance our vision is not quite normal. Usually the two parts of the visual system that are out of balance control the perception of "opposites," so our perception of the test stimulus is the opposite of our perception of the adapting stimulus.

Motion Aftereffect

There is a part of the visual system that is used for seeing motion. This part is divided into several motion detectors and each of these detectors sees motion in only one direction. These motion detectors are arranged in pairs so that each member of a pair sees motion in the opposite direction (for example, one sees upward motion and the other sees downward motion). If we fatigue, or tire out, one member of a pair, then the other takes over temporarily.

Click **Aftereffects** and select **Motion** from the popup menu. If you would like to see more information about this aftereffect, click the **Help** button before you make your selection. First you will see the test stimuli, two grating patterns (take a look at the **Background** information section of the **Spatial Vision** demonstration if you would like to know what a grating pattern is). The grating on the top will drift to the left and the grating on the bottom will drift to the right for about a minute—these are the adapting stimuli. While the patterns are moving, look at the white bar in the middle—*DO NOT* move your eyes or try to follow the moving patterns. When the movement stops, the test stimuli will reappear.

Describe what happens to the test stimuli after the movement stopped. Were they still or did they appear to move? If they moved, did they move in the same direction or different directions? How was the motion of the aftereffect different from the motion of the adapting stimuli?

Size and Orientation Aftereffects

There are also parts of the visual system that are used for seeing size and orientation (tilt). These parts are also divided up into pairs of "opposite" detectors, just like the motion detectors. If we fatigue, or tire out, one member of a pair, then the other takes over temporarily.

View the **Size** and then the **Orientation** aftereffects by selecting them from the **Aftereffects** popup menu. They work just like the motion aftereffect. First you will see the adapting stimuli for about a minute. While the adapting stimuli are being shown, look at the white bar in the middle—*DO NOT* move your eyes or try to follow the moving patterns. Finally, the test stimuli will reappear.

 Describe the size and orientation aftereffects. Compare how the test stimuli looked before and after you viewed the adapting stimuli. Also, compare the top and bottom test stimuli with the top and bottom adapting stimuli for each aftereffect.

Color Aftereffects

The part of our visual system that sees color is also divided up into pairs of "opposite" color detectors. With color detectors, red and green are opposites and blue and yellow are opposites.

Click **Aftereffects** and select **Negative Afterimages** from the popup menu. You will be asked to **Select a color for the adapting image**— select **Red** and click the **OK** button. The adapting image will be shown for about a minute—with this aftereffect, you can look anywhere in the colored part of the screen. The adapting image will then be replaced by the test image—a plain white screen.

 Does the plain white test image appear to have a color tint? What color is it?

Try **Aftereffects: Negative Afterimages** again with a **Green**, then a **Blue**, and then a **Yellow** adapting image. It would be best if you waited a few minutes between each one, so that the previous aftereffect has a chance to wear off.

 What color is the afterimage for each of the adapting colors? Are the aftereffects equally strong for all colors? If not, which colors produce the strongest aftereffects?

The McCollough Effect

The McCollough effect is one of the strongest and longest lasting of all the aftereffects. It is a combination of the orientation and color aftereffects. Click **Aftereffects** and select **McCollough Effect** from the popup menu. There are two different adapting stimuli that you will see—a set of red and black vertical bars and a set of green and black horizontal bars. The two patterns will alternate—you will see each for a few seconds at a time—for a total of about *four minutes*. This aftereffect takes a long time to develop, so please be patient. The adapting stimuli will then be replaced by the test stimulus. The test stimulus is a pattern that has black and white bars—some are horizontal and some are vertical.

Describe the test stimulus. Do the horizontal parts of the test stimulus look different than the vertical parts?

If you have the opportunity, try to see how long it takes for the McCollough effect to wear off. You can go back and look at the McCollough test stimulus without viewing the adapting stimuli again. To do this, click **Aftereffects** and select **Show McCollough Picture** from the popup menu. If you can, try looking at the test stimulus a half hour after you adapted *(DO NOT adapt again)*. Try again after an hour, or even a day or two later.

   Some people report that the McCollough effect lasts for hours or even days. How long did it last for you? Sometimes it's hard to tell where to draw the line between an aftereffect and learning (learning is usually believed to involve a long-term change in the brain). What do you think the McCollough effect is and why?

Miscellaneous

Do a search for illusions or aftereffects on the Web. You should be able to find lots of them.

   Briefly describe the most interesting illusion or other sensory phenomenon that you can find on the Web.

Spatial Vision—Making Waves

OBJECTIVES

By completing this exercise, you will learn about:

- what sine waves are and what they look like.

- how sine waves can differ in frequency and amplitude.

- how sine waves can be used as a graph, or luminance profile, to plot brightness in a grayscale image—what a sine wave grating is.

- how sine waves can be added together to create complex patterns (Fourier synthesis).

GETTING STARTED

Before beginning this exercise go to the **Spatial Vision** demonstration and click the Info button. Read the **Background** information for an introduction to Fourier analysis. Also read "Adding Sine Waves" in the **Instructions** (it's toward the end of the Instructions) for information you will need to operate the program.

INSTRUCTIONS

The following is a brief summary of the program instructions:

- To get to the "Making Waves" portion of the program select **Waves**. For more information click in the **Help** button (it has a question mark on it) and move the mouse around the screen.

- Enter **Frequency** and **Amplitude** values for up to 13 sine waves in the boxes on the right. Frequencies can be up to 250 and amplitudes up to 1000. If you don't want a wave to be added, enter a **Frequency** of 0 or an **Amplitude** of 0 (or delete the frequency or amplitude value).

- The **Square Wave** button fills in the frequencies and amplitudes to approximate a square wave.

- The **Clear** button erases the current sum of waves and sets the frequency and amplitude values of all waves (except the first) to zero.

- The **Plot** button adds up the sine waves then plots the sum and draws the corresponding grating pattern.

EXERCISE

Simple Sine Waves

First you will learn about sine waves—what they look like, how changing their amplitude and frequency change the way they look, and what a sine-wave grating looks like. To do this you will only be plotting one wave at a time, so make sure that the amplitude boxes for all the waves except the first one are either empty or have zeros in them (clicking the **Clear** button will do this for you).

Enter a **Frequency** of 1 and an **Amplitude** of 1000 for the first wave, then click the **Plot** button to see the result. You will see one complete cycle of a sine wave plotted on top, and a sine wave grating pattern on the bottom.

✍ What do you think "one complete cycle" means? How does the grating pattern correspond to the sine wave plot?

Enter a **Frequency** of 2 for the first wave (leave its amplitude at 1000), then click the **Plot** button to see the result. Do the same thing with **Frequencies** of 5, 10, 20, and 50.

✍ Now what do you think a "cycle" is? In your own words, describe how changing the frequency of a sine wave affects the way the wave and the grating pattern look (that is, define "frequency").

Enter a **Frequency** of 5 and an **Amplitude** of 500 for the first wave, then click the **Plot** button to see the result. Do the same thing with **Amplitudes** of 250, 100, 50, 10, and 5.

✍ In your own words, describe how changing the amplitude of a sine wave affects the way the wave and the grating pattern look. (that is, define "amplitude").

Enter a **Frequency** of 1 and an **Amplitude** of 10 for the first wave, then click the **Plot** button to see the result. Do the same thing with **Frequencies** of 2, 5, 10, 20, and 50.

 Can you see the grating pattern when the frequency is set to 1? At which of the frequencies can you see the grating best? Is it true that the bigger something is (the lower the frequency), the easier it is to see? Or do we see middle frequencies better than lower frequencies?

Complex Waves

Now you will see what happens when you add sine waves together. Click the **Square Wave** button. This will fill in the **Amplitudes** and **Frequencies** so that the sum will be a square wave. (This will not be a "true" square wave, but an approximation—to make a *mathematically perfect* square wave you need to keep adding sine waves until the frequency reaches infinity, and we don't have that much time.) Click the **Plot** button to see the result.

 Describe the wave that was plotted and the grating pattern—how is it not perfectly square? What is the relationship between the sine waves used to make a square wave? If you were going to add a 14th wave to the sum, what would its frequency and amplitude be?

Enter a **Frequency** of 0 for the 13th (last) wave (or just delete the frequency value) and click the **Plot** button to see the result without the highest frequency. Next enter a **Frequency** of 0 for the 12th wave and click the **Plot** button. Continue by entering a **Frequency** of 0 for each wave—*except the first one*—and clicking the **Plot** button after subtracting each wave from the sum. Do this one wave at a time from the bottom to the top. Leave the first wave with a **Frequency** of 1.

 Describe how the wave that was plotted, and the corresponding grating pattern, changed as you removed more and more of the components of the square wave.

Click the **Square Wave** button again, but this time multiply each of the frequency values by 10—you can do this by entering 0 to the left of the decimal point in each **Frequency** value . You should now have **Frequency** values of 10, 30, 50, 70, etc. Click the **Plot** button to see the result.

 Describe this wave and the grating pattern. Does the grating pattern look more square? Does it have sharper edges? Why? In other words, what is it that makes edges "sharp"?

Click the **Clear** button to erase everything. Enter a **Frequency** of 2 and an **Amplitude** of 500 for the first wave. Enter a **Frequency** of 4 and an **Amplitude** of 250 for the second wave. (you should now have values in only the top two frequency and amplitude boxes). Click the **Plot** button to see the result.

 Describe this wave and the grating pattern.

Enter a **Frequency** of 6 and an **Amplitude** of 125 for the third wave then click the **Plot** button. Then enter a **Frequency** of 8 and an **Amplitude** of 62.5 for the forth wave and click the **Plot** button. Continue entering values for each wave by entering the next even number for the next **Frequency**, and half the previous amplitude for the next **Amplitude**. Click the **Plot** button after adding each wave.

 How did the shape of this wave change as you added even frequencies?

Spatial Vision—Image Analysis

OBJECTIVES

By completing this exercise, you will learn about:

- how images can be broken down into a set of sine wave components (Fourier analysis).

- how different types of filters operate on the sine wave components of an image.

- what the different sine wave components of an image "look like"—how an image changes when certain components are removed or changed.

- how the world might look to people with different kinds of visual deficits.

GETTING STARTED

Before beginning this exercise go to the **Spatial Vision** demonstration and click the **Info** button. Read the **Background** information for an introduction to Fourier analysis. Also read the **Instructions** for information you will need to operate the program.

INSTRUCTIONS

The following is a brief summary of the program instructions:

- To get to the "Image Analysis" portion of the program, select **Filter**.

- Click on **Original Image** to select an image from the popup menu.

- Select a **Filter Type**—**High Pass**, **Low Pass**, **Band Pass**, or **Notch**. To set the filter cutoff frequencies use the **arrows** below the **Filter Frequencies** image.

- Click the **Filter Image** button to filter an image.

EXERCISE

Analyzing Square Waves

In the **Spatial Vision—Making Waves** exercise, you "built" a square wave from sine waves. Now you're going to take a square wave apart. Click **Original Image** and select **Square Wave** from the popup menu. Select **Filter Type: Low Pass**. Set the **Filter Frequency** to about 90 and enter a **Filter Efficiency** of 100. Click the **Filter Image** button.

✍ Describe the grating pattern. Does it look like any of the gratings you created in the previous exercise?

Reduce the **Filter Frequency** to about 80 and leave the **Filter Efficiency** at 100. Click the **Filter Image** button.

✍ How is this grating pattern different from the previous one? (It is, so go back and re-filter it if you need to refresh your memory.) Does it look like any of the gratings you created in the previous exercise?

Reduce the **Filter Frequency** to about 50 and leave the **Filter Efficiency** at 100. Click the **Filter Image** button.

✍ How would you describe this wave? Does it look like any of the gratings you created in the previous exercise?

✍ Describe what you just did to the square wave by applying the three filters. Think about what a low-pass filter does (which frequencies it removes) and how a square wave is "made."

Analyzing Text

Click **Original Image** and select **Text Medium** from the popup menu. Select **Filter Type: Low Pass**. Adjust the **Filter Frequency** to about 50 and enter a **Filter Efficiency** of 100. Click the **Filter Image** button.

✍ What happened to the text? Can you read it?

Select **Filter Type: High Pass**, adjust the **Filter Frequency** to about 50, and enter a **Filter Efficiency** of 100. Click the **Filter Image** button.

✍ What happened to the text this time? Can you read it?

Select **Filter Type: Notch**. Adjust the **Filter Frequencies** to about 25 and 85 and enter a **Filter Efficiency** of 100. Click the **Filter Image** button.

✍ What happened to the text this time? Can you read it?

✍ What range of frequencies (high, middle, or low) do you think are used most to "build" text? Think about what each of the three filters did to the image (what frequencies did each remove)—after applying which filters could you still read the text.

Filters and Vision

Some medical conditions cause people to lose their vision for only a narrow range of frequencies. For example, cataracts make it harder to see high frequencies, glaucoma and the early stages of Alzheimer's disease make it harder to see low frequencies, and multiple sclerosis can make it harder to see middle frequencies. What do you think the world might look like if you couldn't see high, middle or low frequencies? For this exercise, click **Original Image** and select any of the "face" images from the popup menu (for example, **Adam**, **Lisa**, **Scott**, or **Some Guy**), and open it.

Select **Filter Type: Low Pass**. Adjust the **Filter Frequency** to between 65 and 70 (so you filter out the high frequencies and leave the low and middle ones alone) and enter a **Filter Efficiency** of 100. Click the **Filter Image** button.

✍ What does the image look like without high frequencies? Can you see the overall shape and form (the "global" parts of the image)? Can you see the edges and fine details (the "local" parts of the image)?

Select **Filter Type: High Pass**. Adjust the **Filter Frequency** to between 40 and 45 (so you filter out the low frequencies and leave the middle and high ones alone) and enter a **Filter Efficiency** of 100. Click the **Filter Image** button.

✍ What does the image look like without low frequencies? Can you see the overall shape and form (the "global" parts of the image)? Can you see the edges and fine details (the "local" parts of the image)?

Select **Filter Type: Notch**. Adjust the **Filter Frequencies** to about 25 and 85 (so you filter out the middle frequencies and leave the low and high ones alone) and enter a **Filter Efficiency** of 100. Click the **Filter Image** button.

✍ What does the image look like without middle frequencies? Can you see the overall shape and form (the "global" parts of the image)? Can you see the edges and fine details (the "local" parts of the image)?

Repeat the last three manipulations above, but this time choose one of the other photographic ("non-face") images (for example, **Tree**, **Oil Rig**, **Bread and Cheese**, or **Bricks**).

✍ What does the image look like without high frequencies?

✍ What does the image look like without low frequencies?

✍ What does the image look like without middle frequencies?

Think about the overall effect all these the various manipulations had on the different types of images.

✍ If you had to lose vision in just one range of frequencies (low, medium, or high), which would affect your vision the most? Which do you think would affect your vision least?

ADDITIONAL INVESTIGATIONS

- Repeat the **Analyzing Square Waves** manipulations (see above) on two or more of the sine wave images. What happens to the sine waves as you change the filter frequency? How is the change with different cutoff frequencies different than what happens with the square wave? Why?

- Compare the effects of various filters on vertical, horizontal, and orthogonal (two perpendicular) sine waves. How does the FFT output change? Why?

- Try various settings of the **Subsampled Image** filter on some of the images. Explain what subsampling is. Explain its effect on images in terms of spatial frequency. Compare and contrast it to the other types of filters. Try squinting when you look at a subsampled image. Does it look less "filtered?" Why? (Think about the effect that squinting has on the spatial frequencies you see—its sort of like applying a filter to your vision.)

3D Pictures

OBJECTIVES

By completing this exercise, you will learn about:

- how stereograms can "fool" our visual system into seeing depth.

- what random-dot stereograms are and how they create a perception of form and depth.

GETTING STARTED

Before beginning this exercise go to the **3D Pictures** experiment and click the **Info** button. Read the **Background** information and **Instructions** for additional information you will need to complete the exercise.

INSTRUCTIONS

The following is a brief summary of the program instructions:

- To view a stereogram select **Random Dots**, **Outlines**, or **Pictures**, and then select one of the available stereograms.

- For some stereograms you can set various parameters. To generate and display a stereogram, set the parameters (if they are available) and click the **Draw It** button.

- View the stereograms with the red-green (or red/blue) glasses. The *red* lens goes over your *right* eye.

EXERCISE

Random Dot—Density

Random-dot stereograms are a very special kind of stereogram because we can not only see depth in them, but we also see solid shapes where none exist. Each eye views only a pattern of random dots that has no shape or form (there are no edges). Our brain "creates" the shape by comparing and matching up the dots seen by each eye. There are no monocular cues to depth in a random-dot stereogram—the only depth cue is the disparity of the dots.

Select **Random Dots** and then select **Square**. Enter a **Dot Density** of 98 (that means that, on the average, about half of the dots will be colored), and a **Disparity** of 5 (that means that the difference in the position of the square seen by the left and right eye will be 5 pixels). Enter an **Object Size** (how big the square is) of 100. Click **Draw It** to generate and draw the stereogram. When the stereogram is finished drawing, view it with the red-green (or red/blue) glasses (the *red* lens over your *right* eye). You may need to view these random-dot stereograms for a minute or two before you see anything. View them from directly in front of the monitor at about arm's length, about 55–60 cm (20–24 in).

 Describe what you see. Is the object in front of or behind the screen? Does the object really look like a square? Does it have sharp, distinct edges?

Reversing the glasses (the *red* lens over your *left* eye) reverses the disparity (objects shifted to the right are shifted to the left, and vice-versa). Reverse the glasses and view the stereogram again.

 How does the appearance of the stereogram change when you reverse the glasses?

Select **Random Dots** and then select **Square**. Enter a **Dot Density** of 50—don't change the disparity or object size. Click **Draw It** to generate and draw the stereogram. When the stereogram is finished drawing, switch the glasses back (the *red* lens over your *right* eye) and view it.

 Can you see the square? Does it have sharp, distinct edges?

Try the same thing with **Dot Densities** of 25, 10, and 5. You may need to look at these for a minute or two to get the full effect.

✍ Can you see the square at each of these densities? Does it always have sharp, distinct edges? Do you think it should? Why or why not? Are you surprised by what you see?

Select **Random Dots** and then select **Steps**. Enter a **Dot Density** of 98 and a **Disparity** of 5. Click **Draw It** to generate and draw the stereogram. When the stereogram is finished drawing, view it with the red-green (or red-blue) glasses (the *red* lens over your *right* eye).

✍ Describe what you see.

Reverse the glasses (the *red* lens over your *left* eye) and view the stereogram again.

✍ What does the stereogram look like when you reverse the glasses?

Select **Random Dots** and then select **Steps**. Enter a **Dot Density** of 1. Click **Draw It** to generate and draw the stereogram. When the stereogram is finished drawing, switch the glasses back (the *red* lens over your *right* eye) and view it. You may need to look at this one for a minute or two to get the full effect.

✍ Can you see the steps? Are the black spaces between the dots without depth or do they appear to have the same depth as the neighboring dots? Do you think these blank areas should have depth? Why or why not?

Random Dot—Disparity

Select **Random Dots** and then select **Square**. Enter a **Dot Density** of 98, a **Disparity** of 5, and an **Object Size** of 100. Click **Draw It** to generate and draw the stereogram. When the stereogram is finished drawing, view it with the red-green (or red-blue) glasses (the *red* lens over your *right* eye) at a distance of about 55–60 cm (20–24 in). Do the same with a **Disparity** of 3 and then 1 (that means that the difference in the position of the square seen by the left and right eye will be 3 pixels and 1 pixel). *It is important for this part of the exercise that your viewing distance is the same for each disparity.*

✍ Compare what you see with different disparities? What happened to the square? What is the relation between the depth you perceive and the disparity of the images?

Enter a **Disparity** of 10 (don't change the dot density or object size). Click **Draw It** to generate and draw the stereogram. When the stereogram is finished drawing, view it with the red-green (or red-blue) glasses (the *red* lens over your *right* eye). Do the same with a **Disparity** of 15. *It is important for this part of the exercise that your viewing distance is the same for each disparity.*

✍ What happened to the square? Can you clearly see the depth? There is a limit to the amount of disparity the visual system can use to perceive depth. If the two eyes' views are too different, the visual system cannot combine the images and we see double (diplopia). Did disparities of 10 or 15 exceed this limit?

Stereo Photographs

Stereo photographs are taken with a special camera that has two lenses and takes two pictures at the same time. The lenses are side by side, about the same distance apart as our eyes. As a result, each of the pictures is slightly different, just like the difference between the images seen by our two eyes. Because these pictures are of objects in the "real world," they contain both monocular depth cues and disparity.

Select **Pictures: Vatican** and **Pictures: On Duty**. (You can look at the other stereo photos too, but these two show depth especially well.) View these stereo photos with the red-greed (or red-blue) glasses (the *red* lens over your *right* eye) and without the glasses.

✍   Describe the difference between viewing the stereo photos with and without the glasses.

Reversing the glasses (the *red* lens over your *left* eye) reverses the disparity but not the monocular depth cues. In other words, you are sending your brain mixed signals about depth. Reverse the glasses (the *red* lens over your *left* eye) and view the stereo photos again.

✍   Does the depth reverse in the stereo photos in the same way it does in the random-dot stereograms when you reverse the glasses? Describe how they look with the glasses reversed. Which depth cue(s) "win out"— monocular cues, disparity, or neither?

Color Arrangement Test

OBJECTIVES

By completing this exercise, you will learn about:

- taking and scoring a common test for color vision deficiencies.
- normal color vision and color vision deficiencies.

GETTING STARTED

Before beginning this exercise go to the **Color Arrangement Test** demonstration and click the **Info** button. Read the **Background** information and **Instructions** for additional information you will need to complete the exercise.

INSTRUCTIONS

The following is a brief summary of the program instructions:

- Drag the **color patches** on the bottom to the row of white patches on the top, arranging them so that the most similar patches are next to each other.
- To reposition a **color patch** in the top row, drag it to a new position.
- When you have arranged the patches in the top row to your satisfaction, click the **Score Test** button.
- Click the **Results Table** button to see a numerical analysis, and click the **Results Graphic** button to see a graphical representation of your results.

EXERCISE

The object of this test is to arrange the **color patches** so that the most similar patches are closest to one another. When you begin, the first color patch is already placed at the far left of the top row. From the color patches in the bottom row select the one most similar to the one in the top row and drag it to the second position in the top row. Next, find the color patch on the bottom most similar to the second patch in the top row. Continue dragging patches from the bottom to the top until you have arranged all of the colored patches in order on the top.

 Print both the graphical and numerical results of your test.

 Based on your test results, how would you describe your color vision?

xing demonstration
nformation and
eed to complete

instructions:
hange the amounts
e. The numbers on the
ro means none of that
that color.
lor Mixture patch.
ce.

e a color, the point
after you define a new
clear the colors

you like by clicking
. To reset the **Color**
n.

an, magenta, and
, and blue. A color is
m any combination
screen are produced
ed light (like print
mixing red, green,
a, and yellow are

g **RGB** (below the
5 and the amount

sure you are still

sure you are still

y colors from the
condary colors plotted in
RGB color space?

Be sure you are still viewing the **RGB** color space and adjust the color
mixture to make shades of gray. Make a light gray, a medium gray and a
dark gray.

✍ Describe the general rule for making grays. How does this compare to making white? Where are the grays plotted in the RGB color space?

Brightness

Select **RGB** (below the **Color Space**). Pick one of the primaries (**Red**, **Green**, or **Blue**), set its value to 255 and set the values of the other two primaries to 0. Click the **Remember** button to save this setting. Now decrease the amount of the primary you picked to 200 and click the **Remember** button again. Continue decreasing the amount of the primary you picked by 50, clicking the **Remember** button each time, until you reach zero. For example, if you picked **Red**, your settings would be done as follows:

Red: 255	Red: 200	Red: 150	Red: 100	Red: 50	Red: 0
Green: 0	Green: 0	Green: 0	Green: 0	Green: 0	Green: 0
Blue: 0	Blue: 0	Blue: 0	Blue: 0	Blue: 0	Blue: 0
Remember	Remember	Remember	Remember	Remember	Remember

Repeat this entire process for each of the other two primary colors.

✍ Describe how brightness is plotted in the RGB color space (it may help to rotate the the **Color Space** to get a view from different angles).

Now select **HSB** below the **Color Space**.

✍ Describe how brightness is plotted in the HSB color space.

Click the **Forget** button to clear your color settings, and be sure you are still viewing the **HSB** color space. Set **Red** to 255 (its maximum) and set **Green** and **Blue** to 0. Click the **Remember** button. Now do the same for **Green**, then **Blue**, clicking the **Remember** button each time. Your settings should be done as follows:

Red: 255	Red: 0	Red: 0
Green: 0	Green: 255	Green: 0
Blue: 0	Blue: 0	Blue: 255
Remember	Remember	Remember

You will have three bright, pure primaries plotted in the **Color Space**.

✍ Where are these three points located relative to the height of the axis? Are they in the white, gray, or black zone?

Now rotate the **Color Space** to view it from the top (the axis should be a small point).

✍ Describe the location of the three primaries in the color space, relative to each other and to the axis.

Saturation

Click the **Forget** button to clear your previous color settings and select **HSB** below the **Color Space**. Pick one of the primaries (**Red**, **Green**, or **Blue**), set its value to 255 and set the values of the other two primaries to 0. This creates a saturated, or pure, color. Click the **Remember** button to save this setting. Now adjust the amounts of the other two colors to 42 and click the **Remember** button to save this new setting. Continue adding to the other two colors in equal amounts (add about 42 or 43) and saving each setting until you reach 255. So, while one of the colors stays set at 255, the other two colors should be set to about 42, 84, 127, 169, 212, and 255. It is not important to use these exact values—*it IS important to set the values for each of the other two colors the same.*

How did the appearance of the color mixture change as it became less and less saturated? How did the position of the colors in the HSB color space change? Describe in your own words what is meant by saturation.

Hue

Click the **Forget** button to clear your previous color settings and select **HSB** below the **Color Space**. Create and **Remember** the three primary colors (red, green, and blue) by setting one color's value to 255 and the other two colors' values to 0 for each primary color. Next, create and **Remember** the three secondary colors (cyan, magenta, and yellow). Your settings should be done as follows:

Red: 255	**Red:** 0	**Red:** 0	**Red:** 0	**Red:** 255	**Red:** 255
Green: 0	**Green:** 255	**Green:** 0	**Green:** 255	**Green:** 0	**Green:** 255
Blue: 0	**Blue:** 0	**Blue:** 255	**Blue:** 255	**Blue:** 255	**Blue:** 0
Remember	Remember	Remember	Remember	Remember	Remember

You should now have six colors plotted in the HSB color space.

How should now have six colors plotted in the HSB color space.

Describe the positions of the three secondary colors relative to the three primary colors. (It would probably be best to view the color space from the top to see the positions of these colors.) Are they located where you would expect them to be? Why or why not? Describe in your own words how hue is represented in the HSB color space.

Hue, Saturation & Brightness

Click the **Forget** button to clear your previous color settings and select **HSB** below the **Color Space**. Adjust the color settings to make black.

What are the red, green, and blue settings you used to make black? Where is black in the HSB color space?

Adjust the color settings to make an orange color.

What are the red, green, and blue settings you used to make orange?

Adjust the color settings to make a pink color.

What are the red, green, and blue settings you used to make pink? Is your pink created with only one primary color, only one secondary color, or a combination of colors? Which hues did you use? Is your pink saturated or desaturated? Is it bright or dark?

Brown is a tricky color to make. Adjust the color settings to make a brown color. (Be sure you are still viewing the **HSB** color space.)

What are the red, green, and blue settings you used to make brown? Where is your brown in the HSB color space? Is it a bright or a dark color?

Some colors are difficult to make, especially colors that we say are "metallic." Adjust the color settings to make a gold color.

Is it possible to make the color gold? If so, what are the red, green, and blue settings you used to make gold? If not, what other factors might contribute to our perception of the color gold?

Subtractive Color Mixing

Click the **Forget** button to clear your previous color settings, and select **CMY** below the **Color Space**. This will change the primary colors to **Cyan**, **Magenta**, and **Yellow**, the colors used in subtractive color mixing. Adjust the color settings to make black.

✍   What are the cyan, magenta, and yellow settings you used to make black? Where is black in the CMY color space?

Adjust the color settings to make white.

✍   What are the cyan, magenta, and yellow settings you used to make white? Where is white in the CMY color space?

Adjust the color settings to make the three secondary colors. (Be sure you are still viewing the **HSB** color space.)

✍   Is the relationship between primary and secondary colors the same for additive and subtractive color mixing?

✍   Compare the mixtures that make black and white in additive color mixing to the mixtures that make black and white in subtractive color mixing. Describe the most significant difference between additive and subtractive color mixing.

Mach Bands and Simultaneous Contrast

OBJECTIVES

By completing this exercise, you will learn about:

- the concepts of brightness and luminance, and that the two are not always the same.

- what Mach bands are and what they tell us about the visual system.

- the concept of lateral inhibition and how neighboring cells communicate with on another.

GETTING STARTED

Before beginning this exercise go to the **Mach Bands** demonstration and click the **Info** button. Read the **Background** information and **Instructions** for additional information you will need to complete the exercise. You will also be using the **Illusions and Aftereffects** demonstration to do this exercise.

INSTRUCTIONS

Simultaneous Contrast

- To view an illusion in the **Illusions and Aftereffects** demonstration click **Motion**, **Depth**, **Contrast**, **Size**, **Shape**, **Orientation**, **Bistable**, or **Misc** and select an illusion from the popup menu.

- For information about individual illusions or aftereffects click the **Help** button (it has a question mark on it). When Help is turned on, you will see information about each illusion before you view it. Reviewing this information may help you answer some of the questions below.

Mach Bands

- Click the **arrow** buttons to plot and erase the **Luminance Profile**. A *plot* of the luminance profile is shown in a graph at the top of the screen and a *grayscale* luminance profile is shown below it. Click the **Clear** button to erase the **Luminance Profile**.

- Enter values for **Amplitude** and **Space Constant** to set the amount and spread of inhibition.

- Click the **Calculate** button to show the perceptual equivalent of the **Luminance Profile** that you have plotted.

EXERCISE

Simultaneous Contrast

Go to the **Illusions and Aftereffects** demonstration. Click **Contrast** then select **Simultaneous Contrast—Static** from the popup menu.

✍ Describe the brightness of the gray spot on the left compared to the brightness of the gray spot on the right.

Click **Contrast** then select **Simultaneous Contrast—Dynamic** from the popup menu. This illustrates the same concept as the previous illusion, but the effect is much more dramatic.

✍ Does the brightness of the spot change as it moves across the background? If so, describe how it changes.

The change in the spot's brightness is an illusion—the spot doesn't really change. To demonstrate this select **Black Background** or **White Background** to show the spot on a solid background. Select **Shaded Background** to show the spot on a shaded background.

✍ Based on the demonstrations of static and dynamic simultaneous contrast, describe a general rule that relates the brightness of an object to the brightness of the background on which it is viewed.

✍ Based on the simultaneous contrast effect, which type of information would appear to be most relevant to our perception, absolute brightness or relative brightness?

Mach Bands

Go to the **Mach Bands** demonstration. A *plot* of the luminance profile is shown in a graph at the top of the screen and a *grayscale* luminance profile is shown below it. Use the **arrow** buttons to plot a **Luminance Profile** that contains both a smooth gradient and sharp steps—something like that shown below.

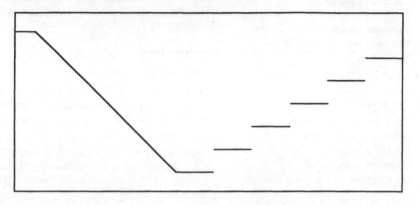

✍ Compare the plot of the luminance profile to the grayscale luminance profile. Are they the same? In other words, does the grayscale luminance profile look like you would expect based on its graph?

Mach Bands are areas that seem brighter or darker than they really are. They are caused by a phenomenon called **lateral inhibition**.

✍ Do you find any bright Mach Bands in the luminance profile? Where are they located?

✍ Do you find any dark Mach Bands in the luminance profile? Where are they located?

Make sure that the **Amplitude** of inhibition is set to 0.90 and click the **Calculate** button. The white line is a graphical representation of how the luminance profile would appear to a visual system with lateral inhibition.

✍ Is the plot of the luminance profile shown by the white line similar to your perception of the grayscale luminance profile?

Now set the **Amplitude** of inhibition to 0 (no lateral inhibition). Click the **Calculate** button and compare the plot of the luminance profile (white line) to the grayscale luminance profile.

✍ What amount of lateral inhibition generates a plot of the luminance profile that most closely approximates the grayscale luminance profile— 0 or 0.90?

✍ Based on your observations, did your visual system demonstrate lateral inhibition?

Clear the display by clicking the **Clear** button and plot a **Luminance Profile** with one large step, as shown below. Enter an **Amplitude** of inhibition of 0.90 and click the **Calculate** button.

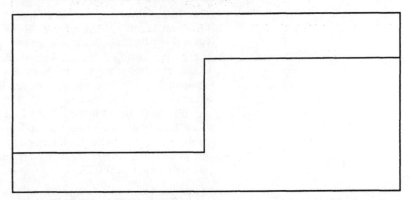

 When a light area is next to a dark area, where do the bright Mach Bands appear, on the light area or the dark area?

 What aspect of a luminance profile is most affected by lateral inhibition, sharp edges or gradual gradients?

 Describe the perceptual function served by lateral inhibition? In other words, how does lateral inhibition help us see?

ADDITIONAL INVESTIGATIONS

Create other **Luminance Profiles** that demonstrate Mach bands. Can you create any that work better than the examples in this exercise? If so, describe it/them. What characteristic(s) should be part of the profile to get the best Mach band effect?

Scaling Vision

CREATING SCALES

The scaling of perceptions is a topic that has interested vision scientists for about as long as there have been vision scientists (that's over 150 years now!). A scale is something that is used to compare or measure things. For example, we use a scale of inches and feet to measure the size of things. Measuring the size of objects in the real world is pretty simple compared to creating a scale that can be used to measure vision. If the **actual** size of something is 6 inches, then something that is twice as long will obviously be 12 inches. But when you measure the apparent size of something, things are more complicated. An object that is twice as big as another doesn't always look twice as big. That's why scientists who study vision (and the other senses) have spent so much time thinking of ways to create perceptual scales.

Many psychophysical procedures have been developed for constructing scales of **apparent magnitude**. All of these procedures ask observers to make quantitative judgments of subjective (perceptual) events. One of the most direct methods of measuring the apparent magnitude of a stimulus is called **magnitude estimation**. In a magnitude estimation procedure the observer assigns numbers to a group of stimuli so that the numbers represent the apparent magnitudes of the stimuli. When the observer has assigned numbers to a range of stimuli, a scale can be created that measures the observer's perception of those stimuli.

Usually, the observer uses a stimulus called the **standard** to compare to the other stimuli. The standard is assigned a number by the experimenter, then observers assign numbers to the other stimuli to show how they compare to the standard. For example, if the standard has a value of 100 and another stimulus looks twice as big, the observer would assign the value 200 to it. If another stimulus looks half as big, the observer would assign the value 50 to it. As you may have noticed, this is a very straightforward way of creating a scale for apparent magnitude. It's also a very versatile procedure—not only can it be used to scale apparent size, but it can be applied to almost any kind of perception, like brightness, speed, loudness, pitch, hardness, or sweetness.

TYPES OF SCALES

Over the years, vision scientists have learned that different types of perceptions produce different types of scales. The difference between these scales is in how apparent magnitude changes with actual magnitude. One possible relation between actual magnitude and apparent magnitude is **linear**. A linear relation means that both actual and apparent magnitude grow at the same rate. For example, when something really is twice as big, it "appears" to be twice as big. When you plot a linear relation on a standard graph, the function is a straight line. This means that the difference between magnitudes is the same on all parts of the scale. For example, when the difference in length between two lines is 5 inches, this difference should appear the same whether the lines are 10 and 15, 50 and 55 inches, or 100 and 105 inches.

However, visual scales are usually not this simple—**the visual system is usually not linear**. For example, think about how brightness changes when you first switch on a three-way light bulb, and then switch the bulb to its brighter settings. When you enter a dark room and first turn on the light to the 50 watt setting, you see a large change in brightness. If you then turn the switch to the 100 watt setting, you see another change in brightness, but it doesn't seem to be nearly as much of a change as when you first turned on the light. In both cases, the change in wattage is 50: 0 to 50 watts the first time and 50 to 100 watts the second time. Now imagine switching the bulb from the 100 to the 150 watt setting. Again, there is a change of 50 watts, but the increase in the brightness that you see is much less than what you noticed when you first turned on the bulb, or even when you switched the bulb from 50 to 100 watts. Many visual scales work in this way and are not linear—**the bigger something is, the bigger the change you need in order to see the same difference**. Ernst Weber (pronounced VAY-BER) first suggested this type of scale in 1843.

A **logarithmic function** (log function for short) can describe (mathematically) the finding that large changes are needed to see the difference when the stimuli are already large. When you plot a log function on a standard graph, it starts out steep, then flattens out as the numbers get bigger. So when the light is dim, an increase of 50 watts is a big visual change (the steep part of the graph). But when the light is already bright, an increase of 50 watts doesn't look as different (the flat part of the graph). If you plot a log function on a different kind of graph, called a semi-log graph (logarithms on one axis and linear numbers of the other axis), a log function is a straight line. That's because on a log scale the smaller numbers are more spread out than the larger numbers. The higher you go up a log scale, the closer together the values get. A German scientist named Gustav Fechner (pronounced FECK-NER) was one of the first to suggest that many visual scales are log functions (that was in 1860).

Another type of scale that is similar to a log function is the power function. When you plot a power function on a standard graph, sometimes it curves upward and sometimes it curves downward. If you plot a power function on a log graph (logarithms on both axes), it is a straight line. This type of scale was first suggested by an American perceptual scientist named S.S. Stevens in the 1950s. Log and power functions are similar in that lower values are spread out and higher values are closer together. **The difference** between log and power functions is in **how much** the small values are spread out, and in **how much** the larger values are closer together.

SCALING IN THE VISUAL SYSTEM

Each of these three types of scales (linear, log, or power) could be used by the visual system to measure the magnitude of stimuli. To find out which of these three scales best describes a particular visual perception (like size or brightness), you can do an experiment that uses the magnitude estimation procedure described above. The data you get from the magnitude estimation procedure can then be plotted on the three types of graphs— linear, semi-log, and log. If the results look like a straight line when plotted on a linear graph, then you can conclude that processing of magnitude in the visual system is best described with a linear scale. If the results look like a straight line when plotted on a semi-log graph, then you can conclude that processing of magnitude in the visual system is best described with a log scale. If the results look like a straight line when plotted on a log graph, then you can conclude that processing of magnitude in the visual system is best described with a power scale. Luckily, there are statistical analyses that can be performed to determine which function has the straightest line, so you don't have to guess ("eyeball" it) which of the three functions works best. Statistics give us a quantitative way to judge the results of an experiment.

Measuring Illusions

The visual system provides us with very accurate information about the world around us and very rarely makes mistakes. You have to look pretty hard to find examples of when the visual system is inaccurate. When the visual system provides information about our surroundings that is inaccurate, it is called an **illusion**. Vision scientists are very interested in visual illusions for two reasons. First, because the visual system is usually so accurate, it is rare to find cases where it makes a mistake. And second, if we can understand why the visual system was fooled into making a mistake, then we can begin to understand how the visual system processes complex and ever-changing information to provide an accurate, stable perception of the world around us.

This is the biggest challenge to the visual system—to find a rule or strategy to use that permits it to generate an accurate and stable perception of a constantly-changing world. If we never moved, or if the world never moved or changed, then the visual system's job would be easy. But we do move, and the world is always changing, and this is what makes it difficult for the visual system to find the right rules and use them at the right times. For example, at arm's length look at the finger nail on the thumb of your left hand and at the finger nail on the little finger of your right hand. You will notice that your thumb nail is larger than your little finger nail. What rule might the visual system use to decide that your thumb nail is larger than your finger nail? A simple rule would be: **the larger the image on the retina**, the larger the object is. However, if the visual system used this simple rule it would make many mistakes in a world where the objects, and you, move back and forth. For example, look again at the finger nail on the little finger of your right hand, and compare it to the size of the thumb nail on your left hand. But this time move your right hand about six inches from your face, and keep your left hand at arm's length. Does your thumb nail still appear bigger than your finger nail, even when your thumb is farther away? If the visual system used the simple "size of the image on the retina" rule to calculate size, your visual system would tell you that your finger nail is larger—because its image on your retina will be larger when it is much closer. Of course, this would be wrong, because your thumb nail is really larger. In this case, your visual system "knows" that your thumb nail is really larger, even though the size of the two images on the retina would indicate the opposite. What this tells us is that the visual system must use a different rule to represent the size of objects—a rule that takes into account how far away something is (in addition to the size of its retinal image). In other words, the visual system must use a rule that includes how far the object is so it can correct for changes in the size of the retinal image as your viewing distance changes.

Many illusions that you will see are caused by tricking the visual system about how far away objects are. By tricking the visual system about distance, we see objects appear to be different sizes when in fact they are the same size. We learn then that the visual system does use information about the distance of an object to help it process information about the size of an object. What is important to remember is that the rules the visual system use work **almost** all the time—the visual system gives us accurate information about our surroundings even though our surroundings are always changing. It's only when the visual system is tricked that the rules don't work, and the visual system gives us inaccurate information about the world.

Global Precedence

PARALLEL PATHWAYS

There are two main pathways that carry information from the eyes to the brain—the P pathway and the M pathway. Each of these pathways serves different functions and carries different kinds of information to the brain. This parallel processing system is a very efficient way of doing things, because the two pathways can each process different types of visual infomation at the same time.

The **parvocellular**, or P, pathway carries information mainly from the center of the retina, the area where the image falls when you look directly at something. The information it carries is about small things, the fine detail in an image (the **local** parts of an image). Of the two, the P pathway is slower at getting information to the brain.

In contrast, the **magnocellular**, or M, pathway carries information mainly from around the center of the retina, your peripheral vision. It carries information about larger things, the overall shape and form of an image (the **global** parts of an image). The M pathway is the faster of the two at getting information to the brain.

As you can imagine, the world looks pretty different to the two pathways. But these two very different views are combined in the brain to form what we see as a normal image of the world.

GLOBAL PRECEDENCE

Because the visual system is designed in this way, some information is processed faster than other information. The general rule is that processing **time decreases as size increases** (an **inverse** relationship). In other words, information about the global parts of an image gets to the brain before information about the local parts of an image.

One way of showing this difference in speed is by measuring reaction times (RTs) to objects of different sizes. RT measures how long it takes from the time a stimulus is displayed to when an observer can make a response (like pressing a button). It has been shown that RTs tend to be longer to smaller things (for example, a set of narrow stripes, such as a high-frequency grating pattern) than to larger things (for example, a set of wide stripes, a low-frequency grating pattern). This is called the **global precedence effect**, and it means that global information **precedes** local information to the brain. In other words, the visual system seems to process information about **the forest before the trees**.

One question you might ask is (if you were a vision scientist, that is): If you can show this effect with shapes that have no meaning (grating patterns), can you also show it with meaningful shapes (like letters)? This question was first asked by Navon in 1977. In Navon's task, observers were shown large letters made up of smaller letters. The large and small letters were either **consistent** or **inconsistent** with each other. For example, observers may be shown a large, composite H or S constructed from a number of small H's or S's. In the **global condition** observers are instructed to respond as soon as they can identify the larger letter as either an H or S. In the **local condition** they must identify the small, component H's or S's.

This experiment is identical to that performed by Navon. It was designed to answer the question asked above, "Can you show the **global precedence effect** with letters?" The very same experiment can also be used to answer other questions as well. For example, do you think the brain will process the information faster when the global and local letters are the same (**consistent**), or when they are different (**inconsistent**)? You could even combine the questions and ask, for example, is global information processed faster when the letters are consistent or inconsistent?

Feature Analysis

FEATURE ANALYSIS

The analysis of visual information by the brain is a very complex process (even though it happens very quickly). Most vision scientists agree that simple features, or **primitives**, are analyzed in an early stage of this process. One theory that describes this process is Anne Treisman's **feature integration theory**. According to this theory, object perception occurs according to a sequence of stages. In the first stage, called the **preattentive stage**, the visual system analyzes the image and determines the existence of the features that are the basic units, or building blocks, of perception. It has been suggested by some that the analysis of features in the preattentive stage occurs in **parallel**. Some examples of these features are curvature, orientation, ends of lines, color, and movement. In the second stage, called the **focused attention stage**, the features are combined to produce a perception. It has been suggested that the analysis of features in the focused attention stage occurs **serially**.

A visual search task can be used to distinguish between features analyzed in the two stages. In a search task the observer tries to find a target item among several distractors. The observer responds by indicating whether or not they detect the presence of the target. The time it takes the observer to respond is called the **reaction time**, or **RT**.

If the target stimulus has features that are differ from those of the distractors (for example, a target "O" among "V" distractors) then the target stimulus is immediately obvious, and the observer identifies it very rapidly. This rapid identification effect is called **pop-out** because the target literally appears to pop-out of the display. It does not depend on the number of distractors. In other words, RTs are about the same when finding a target among 2 distractors as among 50 distractors. Similar RTs regardless of the number of distractors can be explained within the context of parallel processing—the visual system "looks at," or processes, all the items in a display at the same time.

In contrast, if the target stimulus shares features with the distractors (for example, a target "Q" among "R" and "P" distractors) then pop-out does not occur, and the observer must search the display. In this case, serial processing is involved and that requires focused attention. This means that the observer must scan each item in the display to determine if the target is present. As a result, RTs tend to get longer as the number of distractors increases. In other words, since the visual system can "look at" only one item at a time, it takes longer to find the target among 50 distractors than it does to find it among only 2 distractors.

Unfortunately, as is often the case when we are trying to figure out how our brain works, things are not always so simple. For example, researchers have discovered that search times can be quite a bit different with **exactly the same stimulus** items when the roles of target and distractor are reversed. This effect has been called a **search asymmetry**. For example, it takes less time to find a circle with a line in it (like the letter "Q") among plain circles (like the letter "O") than it does to find a plain circle among circles with lines. The stimuli are the same, the only difference is which one is the target and which one is the distractor. This type of search asymmetry suggests that **parallel processing** is used when the target is distinguished by the presence of a unique feature, and **serial processing** is used when the target is distinguished by the **absence** of a feature present in the distractors. In other words, when you are looking for something to be there, you are faster than when you are looking for something not to be there.

MORE ABOUT FEATURE ANALYSIS

If you want to know more about feature analysis, read on...
(This material is not necessary to complete this exercise.)

Bela Julesz did some of the first research on how we perceive preattentive features. He called these features textons, and believed that they are the basic building blocks of texture perception. It's sort of like the way we see color. That is, the entire spectrum of visible colors can be created with the combination of only three primary colors. Likewise, complex textures can be perceived from the combination of a few simple textons. According to Julesz, the characteristics of textons can be summarized very simply. Textons are: (1) elongated **blobs**—for example, rectangles, ellipses, line segments with specific colors, tilts, widths, etc., (2) **terminators**, or ends of line segments, and (3) **crossings** of line segments. Any complex texture can be made up of combinations of simple textons.

The texton theory of vision is appealing to vision scientists for many reasons. It provides a quantitative framework for making predictions about the detection of new features. In other words, it gives us a way of "measuring" new stimuli and making predictions based on those measurements (that's what a good theory does!). Also, texton theory explains differences in visual search times based on our perception, rather than on explanations based on how we "think," like what strategy we use when we are looking for something. Physiologists like this type of explanation because it makes it much easier for them when they are trying to find the physiological processes responsible for our perception of texture. Trying to find the physiological basis of "thinking" is much more difficult.

Depth Perception

SEEING DEPTH

When we look at the world, we see it in three dimensions (3D)—height, width, and depth. Even though the process of seeing depth is automatic, you don't need to think about it, seeing in depth is not so simple. That's because the depth that we see is created by our brain. Our visual system has no direct way of seeing three dimensions because the images on our retinas are two dimensional (in other words, flat).

One reason that we see depth is that our eyes are about 8-10 cm apart, and each eye views the world from a slightly different position. This slight difference between the images on each retina is used by our visual system to help create a three-dimensional (3D) perception of the world. The difference between the images seen by each eye is called **binocular disparity**. With 3D pictures, or stereograms, a slightly different image is shown to each eye, fooling the visual system into creating a perception of depth where there is none (because the stereograms are flat).

STEREOGRAMS

You may already be familiar with stereograms that can be seen in 3D without glasses—3D posters and books are available everywhere. That type of stereogram is called an **autostereogram**, which can be seen by focusing your eyes behind the image. Some people find this easy to do, but others cannot see them very well or at all. In this demonstration, stereograms are made in a different way, by using two colors to draw the image and viewing the image with special glasses. This type of stereogram, called an **anaglyph**, is made up of red parts and green parts. The glasses have a red filter in one eye and a green filter in the other. The red filter passes the red parts of the image and blocks out the green parts; the green filter passes the green parts of the image and blocks out the red parts. In this way, a different image can be shown to each eye.

MEASURING DEPTH PERCEPTION

Binocular disparity is a measure of the amount of difference between the images seen by each eye. If the difference between the two images is relatively small (the disparity is small), we perceive a single image in depth. This is called **fusion** and is what usually occurs in real life. As the amount of binocular disparity increases, so does our perception of depth. In other words, more disparity means more depth. But, if binocular disparity becomes too large, we can't fuse the images and we experience double vision, or **diplopia**.

In the real world, binocular disparity is determined by the position of objects relative to the point of fixation (the point you're looking at). There is an area in space, called the **horopter**, that is defined by an imaginary circle that passes through each pupil and the point of fixation. From any point on the horopter, the image on each retina will be exactly the same—no disparity. Surrounding the fixation point and the horopter is another region called **Panum's fusional area**. We perceive other objects within Panum's fusional area as being fused (single vision) and standing out in depth relative to the point of fixation. We experience diplopia (double vision) for objects outside of Panum's fusional area. However, if an object is not too far outside, we can perceive it in depth, even though we cannot fuse its images, and we cannot judge the depth very accurately.

In this experiment, you will see how your perception of depth changes with binocular disparity. You will also find out how much disparity is needed for you to experience diplopia. This will give you a measure of Panum's fusional area.

Contrast Sensitivity

When an optometrist tests our vision by having us read a row of black letters on a white chart, what is being measured is our **visual acuity**. Acuity is a measure of one aspect of contrast sensitivity—the upper limit for detecting fine detail at high contrast. However, much of what we see in the real world has a much lower contrast and has an overall shape and form in addition to its fine detail. When we measures an observer's ability to detect objects of different sizes at lower contrasts, the result we plot is called a **contrast sensitivity function** (CSF). The advantage of measuring a CSF, as opposed to a simple measure of acuity, is that it describes how the visual system performs at lower contrasts and at a range of spatial frequencies. Acuity only measures how the visual system performs at high contrast and high spatial frequencies.

One way of indicating the size of an object is in terms of the size of its image on the retina, typically in degrees of visual angle. With patterns that repeat, such as a sinewave grating pattern, size is specified in terms of the number of cycles per degree of visual angle (c/deg). This is a measure of the pattern's **spatial frequency**. A cycle consists of one complete pair of light-dark bars; the example contains 4 cycles. **Lower spatial frequencies** correspond to **wider bars** and **higher spatial frequencies** correspond to **narrower bars**. **Contrast** refers to the difference in luminance between the lightest and darkest points in a cycle. A high-contrast pattern has a large difference between the lightest and darkest parts, for example, black and white. A low-contrast pattern has a small difference between the lightest and darkest parts, for example, two similar shades of gray. (For more information about grating patterns and spatial frequency, look at the "Background" section of the "Spatial Vision" demonstration.)

A CSF is typically generated by measuring an observer's **contrast detection threshold** for a number of different spatial frequencies. The contrast detection threshold is the **lowest contrast at which a pattern can be seen. Sensitivity** is the **reciprocal** of the threshold—the lower your threshold, the higher your sensitivity. A CSF is a plot of contrast sensitivity versus spatial frequency. One interesting thing about the CSF is that it peaks at middle spatial frequencies, about 3-4 c/deg. In other words, when contrast is low we are best able to detect medium-sized objects. As you might expect, we don't see smaller objects as well as medium-sized objects. The smallest objects that we can detect are around 50 c/deg, and they can only be detected if their contrast is very high. What is somewhat surprising at first is that we also **don't see larger objects as well** either. It's not surprising that we are less sensitive to high spatial frequencies since our eyes, like all optical systems, tend to reduce the contrast of high spatial frequencies. However, our eyes do not reduce the contrast of low spatial frequencies. That means that our relative insensitivity to low spatial frequencies is caused by the way the brain processes visual information, rather than by the optics of the eye.

The measurement of acuity provides only **one point on the CSF**. The CSF provides a more valid test of visual performance in the real world. This is especially important since a number of visual deficiencies can affect perception of low-contrast, middle- and low-spatial frequency stimuli without affecting acuity. For example, glaucoma and the early stages of Alzheimer's disease produce a reduced sensitivity to low spatial frequencies, and multiple sclerosis produces a reduced sensitivity to intermediate spatial frequencies. (For more information about the contribution of different spatial frequencies to our visual world, look at the "Spatial Vision" demonstration.)

Signal Detection

SIGNAL DETECTION THEORY

Signal detection theory (SDT) provides a framework within which the sensitivity of sensory systems can be <u>objectively</u> measured and quantified. SDT assumes that all stimuli are added to a background of noise and that the <u>observer's</u> sensory system must be able to tell the difference between the stimulus, called the **signal**, and the **noise**. One source of <u>noise</u> is external, in the environment, but more important to SDT is internal noise, in the sensory system. The main source of internal noise is <u>spontaneous neural activity</u>. Because the internal noise level varies from time to time, a particular stimulus is not always equally detectable. The more noise, the more difficult it is to detect a stimulus. Experiments based on SDT provide a measure of the **minimum stimulus strength necessary to be detected by the observer some proportion of the time**. This is in contrast to classical threshold theories which assume that a particular stimulus is either detectable or not. Threshold theories assume that variability in an observer's responses is the result of imprecise measurement techniques and is not necessarily caused by noise in the sensory system.

RESPONSE CRITERION

In addition to noise, an observer's **response criterion** can also affect their performance in a signal detection task. <u>Response criterion</u> can be influenced by the requirements of the measurement task. If it is more important to the observer to detect the stimulus when it is present (a **hit**) than to avoid saying it is present when it is not (a **false alarm**), then response criterion would be relatively low. In other words, the observer would say they detected the stimulus more often. If, however, it is more important to know when the stimulus is not present (a **correct rejection**) than to fail to detect it when it is present (a **miss**), then criterion would be higher. In other words, the observer would say they **did not** detect the stimulus more often. Because the importance of the observer's response criterion is part of SDT, most signal detection experiments vary either the probability a stimulus will **not** be present (a trial with no stimulus is called a **catch trial**) or the relative payoff/penalty for each type of response. By bringing the observer's response criterion under experimental control, a criterion-free measure of sensitivity can be obtained.

RESPONSE DISTRIBUTIONS

A signal detection experiment produces a value, <u>**d'**</u> (pronounced <u>**d-prime**</u>), which is a measure of the observer's ability to distinguish between the noise alone (**N**) and the signal added to the noise (**S+N**). It is assumed that N and S+N are each represented by a <u>normal response probability distribution</u>. The value d' is the difference between the mean of these two distributions—a measure of sensitivity. Sensitivity is affected by two factors: the **distance between the two distributions** (how much they overlap) and their **variability** (how wide they are). The distance between distributions is determined by the strength of the signal and their variability is determined by noise.

<u>Criterion is represented by a point</u> along the response probability continuum above which the observer always says that the signal was detected and below which the observer never reports detecting the signal. Because this point can be controlled by the experimenter, supporters of SDT believe that there is no consistent, absolute detection threshold.

MEASUREMENT TECHNIQUES

When the observer's response criterion is manipulated by means of changing the payoff schedule or the number of catch trials, data must be collected under several criterion conditions to see how sensitivity varies with the observer's criterion. Running all these conditions can take a lot of time. Fortunately it is possible to get an observer to use several criteria at the same time, in a single block of trials. This is done with a **rating scale** procedure. Instead of using a two-alternative response (as in a Yes-No procedure), the observer rates the certainty of their response. By using a rating scale of certainty, the observer maintains a number of criteria simultaneously, so there is no need to collect data under several different criterion conditions. This procedure is consistent with SDT because it assumes that the stimulus is not always clearly detectable. The observer's certainty of detecting a given stimulus varies over time. A rating scale procedure is one way of bringing the observer's response criterion under experimental control. The result is a criterion-free measure of sensitivity.

ROC CURVE

The results of a SDT experiment are usually plotted in a graph called an **ROC** (Receiver Operating Characteristic) **curve**. For each response criterion the **probability of a Hit**, P(Hit), and the **probability of a False Alarm**, P(FA), can be calculated. Each point on the curve plots the values P(Hit) versus P(FA). d' is directly related to the area under the ROC curve—the larger the area under the curve the larger is d'. An area under the ROC curve of 0.5 means chance performance, that the observer was guessing on every trial. As sensitivity increases, SDT predicts that the slope of the function will remain positive but that the curve will become concave downward. In other words, it will bow upward toward the top-left corner of the graph. Other theories, considered classical threshold theories, predict other kinds of changes in the ROC curve with changes in sensitivity. For example, **Blackwell's High-Threshold Model** predicts that as sensitivity increases, the ROC curve will remain a straight line while its slope decreases and its y-intercepts increases.

The example diagram shows two ROC curves typical of those obtained in a signal detection procedure. For comparison, the type of function predicted by a classical threshold theory is also shown. Corresponding points on the two curves represent the same criteria when the signal was relatively easy to detect (larger d') and and when it was more difficult to detect (smaller d'). Notice that the probabilities of a hit and of a false alarm **are directly related**. This means that as criteria become more liberal the observer is more likely to detect the signal when it is present as well as to indicate that the signal is present when it is not. As the criteria become more conservative both the hit rate and the false alarm rate decrease.

Receptive Field Mapping

MAPPING RECEPTIVE FIELDS

Typically, when an experiment is done that involves recording the activity of individual neurons in the visual system, researchers need to identify the type of cell they are recording. One way of classifying a cell is by the characteristics of its **receptive field**. A cell's receptive field is the **area on the retina within which stimulation causes a change in the activity level of that cell**. In other words, each cell has a certain area of the retina from which it receives input. Each visual neuron in the optic nerve (**ganglion cells**, the axons of which make up the optic nerve), the **lateral geniculate nucleus** (LGN), and the **visual cortex** has a particular type of receptive field that can be used to classify that cell. (For more information about the different types of visual cells, take a look at the "About Vision" topic "The Visual System.")

The following procedure is typically used to find and **map** a cell's receptive field: First a subject is needed. The subject must remain perfectly still throughout the entire mapping procedure. The subject is positioned in front of a large screen on which <u>stimuli</u> can be presented. When mapping visual receptive fields the stimulus must be visual—a light of some form. In order to identify and map different kinds of receptive fields, the experimenter needs to be able to change the size and shape of the stimulus. Since a receptive field is unique to a particular cell, a recording electrode must be positioned in or near a cell body or axon in the visual system. One additional requirement is a means of monitoring and recording the cell's responses. Cell responses are usually converted to an audio signal that's played over a loudspeaker so the experimenter can listen during the experiment—each individual action potential, or **spike**, is heard as a brief click or pop. Cell responses are also typically displayed on an oscilloscope during recording and saved for later computer analysis.

All visual cells respond occasionally, even when they are not being stimulated. This is referred to as **spontaneous activity**, since it is not caused, or **evoked**, by a stimulus. When the cell responds to a stimulus, its activity level changes. A cell that is **excited** by a stimulus **increases** its activity over its spontaneous level. This type of response sounds like a series of very rapid clicks or pops, a lot like popcorn popping. A cell that is **inhibited** by a stimulus **decreases** its activity below its spontaneous level. The sound of this type of response is just the opposite—a period of silence. Some cells respond to the **onset** of a stimulus (when a light is turned on), while others respond to the **offset** of a stimulus (when a light is turned off). To complicate things even further, different cells respond to stimuli of different sizes, shapes, colors, and even directions of motion.

The first step in mapping a receptive field is to locate it. Since you know where in the visual system you are recording, you at least know what **type** of stimulus to use (see below). To find the receptive field, you move the stimulus around the screen, turning it on and off, until you hear a response. Once you find the general location, you more precisely map its outline and determine its characteristics. Once you determine whether a cell responds to stimulus onset (or a stimulus entering the field) or offset (or a stimulus leaving the field), the next step is to trace its receptive field outline. For a cell that responds to stimulus onset, move the stimulus toward the field from the right, marking the spots where the cell first responds. Then move the stimulus from the left, top, and bottom. This gives you a rough outline of the cell. For a cell that responds to stimulus offset, move the stimulus outward from the receptive field center. For cells that respond only to stimuli of a certain orientation or direction or speed of movement, the process is a little more difficult.

GANGLION CELL RECEPTIVE FIELDS

Ganglion cell receptive fields are concentric. That means that they are made up of a small circular region (the **center**) surrounded by a larger circular region (the **surround**). On-center ganglion cells respond best when a small spot of light is **turned on** in their center region. Off-center ganglion cells respond best when the light is **turned off** in their center. The response is best when the stimulus just covers the central region of the receptive field (or just covers the surround in the case of an off-surround cell). Stimuli smaller than the center produce a smaller response, as do stimuli large enough to overlap the receptive field's surround. Stimuli large enough to stimulate both the center and the surround produce a smaller response because the surround response counteracts, or **inhibits**, the center response. Another way of saying this is that the two regions are **antagonistic**.

Ganglion cells can also be classified as **sustained** or **transient**. When a sustained cell is stimulated it responds with a high-frequency burst of spikes. The firing rate remains significantly above the spontaneous level as long as the stimulus is present. A transient cell also responds with a high-frequency burst of spikes, but its firing rate quickly returns to its spontaneous level.

LGN RECEPTIVE FIELDS

Like ganglion cells, cells of the lateral geniculate nucleus (LGN) have circular receptive fields that are concentrically organized and antagonistic. LGN cells typically respond either to the onset of a stimulus (an ON response) or the offset of a stimulus (and OFF response). The subregions tend to be mutually inhibitory, which means that activity in the surround inhibits activity in the center. As a result, the best stimulus is a light that just covers the receptive field's center. Unlike ganglion cells however, LGN cells respond only briefly to stimulus onset or offset. They do not continue to respond if the stimulus remains within the receptive field.

CORTICAL RECEPTIVE FIELDS

Receptive fields in the visual cortex are very different from those of ganglion or LGN cells. Cortical cells are typically elongated with side-by-side subregions. Simple cell receptive fields respond differently depending on which of their subregions is stimulated. Some subregions respond to the presense of a stimulus with an increase in their response (marked with a + in the diagram), while other subregions are inhibited by the presense of a stimulus (marked with a - in the diagram). Because the regions are not circular, simple cells respond best to bars, rather than spots, of light. A stimulus with the same orientation as the receptive field will produce the best response. The greater the difference in orientation between the stimulus and the receptive field's orientation, the smaller the response. A stimulus oriented perpendicular to the receptive field will produce little or no response. A simple cell's response is therefore selective for stimulus orientation.

Another type of cortical cell, the **complex cell**, is selective for stimulus orientation **and** direction of movement. The diagram shows how the response of a typical complex cell varies with stimulus orientation and direction of movement. In this example, the best response is to a stimulus that is parallel to the receptive field, moving up and to the right.

Form and Motion

The human visual system has evolved in such a way that motion plays an important part in almost all visual perception. Experiments where an image is held still on the retina show how important motion really is. An image that doesn't move fades and disappears quickly. It is especially amazing that our visual system can create a perception of a three-dimensional (3D) world from only the two-dimensional (flat) images on our retinas! To do this, our visual system uses many different cues to create perceptions of form and depth, including the slight difference between images seen by our two eyes, shading, and texture. However, a very strong perception of form and depth can be experienced on the basis of motion alone.

All it takes is the movement of an image on the retina to produce a perception of depth. You can demonstrate this very easily with a wire coat hanger and a flashlight. Bend the coat hanger into any 3D shape and use the flashlight to cast its shadow on the wall. Now, rotate the coat hanger and watch its shadow. What do you see? Do you see a flat line changing its shape or do you see a 3D object rotating in depth? Either perception is possible, but your visual system prefers to see a solid object rotating rather than a flat object that is changing its shape. This perception of a three-dimensional object from a moving, two-dimensional image is called the **kinetic depth effect**. We experience this effect because human beings have evolved in a world full of objects that move and rotate. In the natural world, objects normally don't change their shape and size (cartoons don't count).

Our ability to see form and depth is so powerful that motion alone, even without form, can be enough. It was mentioned above that the shadow of a coat hanger can cause us to see depth, but the coat hanger doesn't even need to be present for us to see its form and depth. We can see the same strong perception of a coat hanger rotating in depth if only the two end points of the coat hanger are visible. Our visual system "creates" the form of the coat hanger from the motion alone, without any other information. In fact, our visual system can create the perception of a 3D form from any pattern of dots, if the dots are moved as if they are on the surface of a 3D object. Vision scientists say that the visual system creates **structure from motion**: we can see a form where no form exists, only motion.

Some researchers have extended the study of our ability to see form from motion to more complex kinds of motion. One particular kind of motion that we see every day is **biological motion**. Biological motion is what we call the complex patterns of movement produced by humans and animals. Biological motion was first studied in a very clever series of experiments by Johansson (1975). Johansson attached lights to the shoulders, elbows, wrists, hips, knees, and ankles of actors, and then he made movies of the actors moving around in a dark room. All that was visible on the film was the pattern of movements made by the lights. To his great surprise Johansson discovered that as soon as the actors started moving, observers who had never seen the movies before could immediately tell that the lights were attached to "invisible" human beings. Not only could observers tell that the motion was biological, but they could tell the difference between several different types of movements, such as walking, jogging, and dancing. They could even tell whether the actors were men or women. Even when two actors performed a dance, the complex patterns made by the 24 moving spots of light could easily be identified. These and other findings led Johansson to conclude that our ability to construct the kind of complex perceptions just described must be a very important part of visual perception.

Illusions and Aftereffects

ILLUSIONS

Illusions are fun and interesting to look at, but more importantly they can tell us something about the way our visual system works. By discovering ways in which the visual system can be "fooled," we can learn something about the way we see.

Motion Illusions

In the motion illusions, either we see movement where nothing is really moving, or we see something moving differently than it really is.

Depth & Binocular Illusions

In the depth illusions, we see the appearance of depth because of cues that usually signal depth in the real world. In the binocular illusions, different images are shown to each eye.

Color & Contrast Illusions

Most of the color and contrast illusions are caused by differences in color or brightness of nearby areas. We perceive the color or brightness of objects relative to their surroundings. For example, a piece of white paper looks "white" whether we see it indoors in the evening or outdoors in the bright sunlight, even though the actual brightness of the paper may be hundreds of times darker indoors under artificial light.

Size Illusions

Many researchers believe that most size illusions are illusions of perspective. When we see something that is far away, the image it makes on our retina is smaller than if it were near by. Our visual system "knows" this, so we perceive distant objects at their proper size. Many size illusions fool the visual system into "seeing" depth. For example, in the Ponzo illusion the lines on the side look like they are going off into the distance, so our visual system thinks the top line is further away and it appears to be longer.

Shape Illusions

In the shape illusions, lines appear tilted or bent. Some reseachers believe that these illusions are caused by the way the visual system sees corners and angles. Sometimes angles appear to be bigger than they really are, and other times they appear to be smaller. When many angles are placed close together in certain patterns, shapes can appear distorted.

Orientation Illusions

Many orientation (tilt) illusions are also caused by differences between nearby areas. Tilted objects can make other, nearby objects seem more or less tilted than they really are.

Bistable Figures

These aren't really illusions, but they are interesting because they confuse the visual system. "Bistable" means that these figures can look like two different things. You can see either one thing or the other, and make yourself switch between the two, but you can't see both at the same time.

AFTEREFFECTS

Aftereffects can also tell us something about the way our visual system works, but in different way than illusions. As the name implies, aftereffects are seen **after** you look at something. Usually you view a stimulus, the **adapting stimulus**, for a minute or two. The time during which you are viewing the adapting stimulus is called the **adapting period**.

Immediately after the adapting period, you view another stimulus, the **test stimulus**. The test stimulus is usually similar to, but not exactly the same as, the adapting stimulus. After adapting, the test stimulus looks different than it normally would—that's the aftereffect. Most aftereffects last only a few seconds to a few minutes, but some can last hours or days.

So, what is it that the adapting stimulus does to your visual system that makes some things look different afterwards? Many aftereffects are caused by **fatigue**. One particular part of the visual system is "overworked" by the adapting stimulus and it becomes weakened. In a few minutes it recovers, but during the time that part of the visual system is not working at full strength, other parts work a little harder than they normally do. While things are out of balance our vision is not quite normal. Other aftereffects, such as negative color afterimages, occur in the retina and are caused by the depletion of various photopigments. If high quantities of photopigments are used too rapidly they are depleted; there is a delay before they are replaced and our perception returns to normal.

Almost all aftereffects work on "opposite" parts of the visual system.

Negative Afterimages is a color aftereffect—after viewing a particular color, a gray screen looks like the opposite color (opposite to the visual system that is, for example, red and green or blue and yellow are opposite colors).

The **Gray-Scale Ramp** is a change-in-brightness effect. After viewing an adapting stimulus that keeps getting brighter, a test stimulus looks like it is getting dimmer.

The **Motion** aftereffect is sometimes called the "waterfall effect" because it is similar to what happens after you view a waterfall for a few minutes. After viewing something that moves down (or left), things that are standing still look like they are moving up (or right). This is because the part of the visual system that sees movement in one direction becomes fatigued and the part that sees movement in the opposite direction temporarily takes over.

The **Size** and **Orientation (Tilt)** aftereffects are similar to the motion aftereffect. The Size effect works with parts of the visual system that see how big things are, and the Orientation effect works with parts of the visual system that see how things are tilted.

The **Color Contingent Motion** and **Motion Contingent Color** aftereffects are combinations of color and motion aftereffects. In the first the motion aftereffect depends on the color of the stimulus, and in the second the color aftereffect depends on the direction that the stimulus moves.

The **McCollough effect** is one of the most powerful and long-lasting of all aftereffects. It is a combination of color and orientation aftereffects. Opposite colors are seen only in parts of the test stimulus that are tilted at the same angle as the adapting stimuli. It takes several minutes for this effect to build up, but it can last for hours or even days. Because it lasts so long, some researchers believe that it is not a simple aftereffect—the changes produced in the visual system may be a form of learning.

Spatial Vision

FOURIER ANALYSIS

Almost 200 years ago the French mathematician J.B. Fourier made a very important discovery. He found that any visual image (or any complex waveform) can be broken down into a number of very simple building blocks, or components. This process of breaking down an image into its components is now called **Fourier analysis** in his honor and is as important to understanding spatial vision as atomic theory is to understanding chemistry.

You may recall from chemistry or physics that everything is made up of atoms. By putting together the right combination of atoms, you can make any substance you like. The same is true for images, except that instead of building an image with atoms, the visual system uses **sinewaves**. Just as you can describe any substance by listing its atomic components (like H_2O or CO_2), you can describe any image by listing its sinewave components.

SINEWAVES

So, you might ask, how can you build an image out of waves? In order to do this you need to translate the waves into grayscale patterns. Usually, the peaks are drawn as white, the troughs as black, and everything in between as a shade of gray. You can think of a sinewave as a sort of graph that is used to plot brightness. When you plot a sinewave in grayscale the pattern is called a **sinewave grating**. A sinewave grating pattern looks like a row of dark and light stripes with fuzzy edges. The lighter parts of the grating correspond to the higher parts of the wave, and the darker parts of the grating correspond to the lower parts of the wave.

Although sinewaves are all the same shape, they can differ in other ways. The three measures of sinewaves that are discussed here are **frequency**, **amplitude**, and **orientation**.

Frequency, like wavelength, is a measure of the distance between two successive peaks or troughs in the wave. In fact, frequency is the opposite of wavelength—the shorter the wavelength, the higher the frequency. One way to remember this is that frequency is a measure of how often (or how frequently) the wave repeats itself. In images, low frequencies correspond to the big, or global, parts (the overall shape and form), and high frequencies correspond to the small, or local, parts (the fine detail).

Amplitude is a measure of how big the wave is—it is the distance between the peaks and troughs of the wave. A low-amplitude wave is "flatter" than a high-amplitude wave. In a grating pattern as the amplitude increases, the dark bars get darker and the light bars get lighter. As amplitude decreases, both light and dark bars get closer to a medium gray.

Orientation refers to the angle, or tilt of a grating pattern. If the bars are vertical, the orientation would be zero degrees; if the bars are horizontal, the orientation would be 90 degrees.

In order to build an image, you must add together a large number of sinewaves, of all different frequencies, amplitudes, and orientations. But, you were probably wondering, if sinewaves have fuzzy edges, how can you create an image with sharp edges? The answer is that sinewaves with **very high** frequencies must be added to the lower-frequency sinewaves. For example, another type of wave is a square wave, which has sharp edges and can be made by adding together a certain set of sinewaves. To make a square wave, you start with a sinewave of a particular frequency and amplitude. You then <u>add to it</u> a sinewave that is 3 times the frequency and one third the amplitude, one that is 5 times the frequency and one fifth the amplitude, one that is seven times the frequency and one seventh the amplitude, and so on. Do you notice a pattern here? To get a <u>perfect square wave</u> (mathematically speaking, that is), you need to keep going until you have a sinewave of infinitely high frequency and infinitely small amplitude. Luckily, you don't need to go that high for it to "look like" a square wave—our visual system can't see extremely high frequencies.

FILTERING AND VISION

This exercise illustrates two different image filtering techniques. The first is **subsampling**, where an image is divided up into blocks and the grayscale values within each block are averaged. One result of subsampling is that higher frequency components are removed from an image. More and more detail is lost as the block size becomes larger and larger. You can demonstrate this to yourself by squinting and comparing original and subsampled images. Squinting also tends to reduce high frequencies, and so the two images will look more alike. In addition to removing high frequencies, subsampling also **introduces** high frequencies that were not in the original. High frequencies are present in the subsampled image at the edges of the blocks.

The second image filtering technique is called **spatial filtering**. This type of filter takes advantage of the principles of Fourier analysis outlined above. An image is broken down into its sinewave components, some of those components are removed, then the components that are left are put back together.

Some vision scientists believe that our visual system analyzes images in a way that is similar to Fourier analysis. So filtering images in this way can teach us something about the way our visual system works. We can see what the different components of an image look like, and what images look like with certain components removed. For example, removing high frequencies reduces detail—it's what we usually call blur. However, removing low frequencies produces an image that is very different.

This process can also help us to understand how the world might appear to people with various visual problems. There is evidence for neurons in the visual system that respond to narrow ranges of spatial frequencies. If a group of neurons that responds to a particular range of spatial frequencies do not respond, or do not respond normally, the result can be a visual deficit specific to that spatial-frequency range. For example, **glaucoma** and the early stages of **Alzheimer's disease** make it harder to see low frequencies, **cataracts** make it harder to see higher frequencies, and **multiple sclerosis** makes it harder to see middle frequencies.

3D Pictures

When we look at the world, we see it in three dimensions (3D)—height, width, and depth. Even though the process of seeing depth is automatic, and you don't need to think about it, the mechanisms responsible for seeing in depth are not so simple. That's because the depth that we see is created by our brain. Our visual system has no direct way of seeing three dimensions because the images on our retinas are two dimensional (in other words, flat). So our visual system must use these 2D images to create a perception of a 3D world. There are many cues that the visual system can use in this process.

MONOCULAR DEPTH CUES

Monocular means "one eye," so this type of cue for perceiving depth doesn't depend on us having two eyes (more on that below). These cues are familiar to artists because they use them to make their flat paintings appear to have depth. Some of these cues are:

Overlap—When one object blocks your view of part of another object, the object that is blocked is farther away.

Size (in the Field of View)—The farther away something is, the smaller is its image on our retina.

Shading—The shading of an object and the way it casts shadows can tell us about its shape. For example, the outline of a sphere is just a circle on our retina—its shading gives it depth.

Textures & Detail—The farther away something is, the less we can see of its textures and fine details.

Convergence of Parallel Lines—Parallel lines that are perpendicular to our field of view appear to get closer together in the distance. At some point the lines will appear to touch one another.

Atmospheric Perspective—Dust and other particles in the air make distant objects appear "hazy" and their colors look faded. Objects that are very far away often have a blue or purple tint.

BINOCULAR DEPTH CUES

Binocular means "two eyes," so this type of cue for perceiving depth depends on us having two eyes. Because our eyes are about 8–10 cm apart, each eye views the world from a slightly different position. This slight difference between the images on each retina is used by our visual system to help create a three-dimensional (3D) perception of the world. The difference between the images seen by each eye is called **binocular disparity**. With 3D pictures, or stereograms, a slightly different image is shown to each eye, fooling the visual system into creating a perception of depth where there is none (because the stereograms are flat). Stereograms accompish this by duplicating the images that would occur on the retinas if we were observing a 3D scene.

STEREOGRAMS

In this demonstration stereograms are made by using two colors to draw the two images and viewing the imagse with special glasses. This type of stereogram, called an **anaglyph**, is made up of red parts and green parts. The glasses have a red filter in one eye and a green filter in the other. The red filter passes the red parts of the image and blocks out the green parts; the green filter passes the green parts of the image and blocks out the red parts. In this way, a different image can be shown to each eye.

RANDOM-DOT STEREOGRAMS

Random-dot stereograms are a special type of stereogram made up of two sets of randomly-placed, small dots. For most dots, there is a red dot in one image that is an exact match with a green dot in the other image. There is also a group of dots in one image that is <u>shifted either to the right or left</u> relative to the positions of the matching dots in the other image. This shift in position of some of the dots creates a difference, or **disparity**, between the images seen by the two eyes. When viewed with the red-green glasses, this group of shifted dots appears to "float" in depth above the rest of the background dot pattern. The more the dots are shifted, the greater the disparity and the "higher" above the background the image appears to float. If you reverse the glasses, so each eye sees the other image, the disparity is reversed and the object appears to be behind the background.

This type of pattern is especially interesting to vision scientists because when you view a random-dot stereogram with only one eye, all you see is a <u>random pattern of dots</u>. There is no form or monocular depth cues in either of the patterns alone. The form is "created" by the visual system, which performs the complex calculations needed to match up the dots viewed by each eye and create the perception of a form where no form exists. Random-dot stereograms demonstrate that depth perception can occur when disparity is the **only** depth cue available.

Color Arrangement Test

Much of the early research on how color vision works was based on studies of people with different kinds of color vision deficiencies. There are several different kinds of color deficiencies, and most of these are produced by the absence or abnormality of one or more of the photopigments in the retina. You can tell the type of deficiency by the colors, or wavelengths of light, that the person confuses.

In the rarest type of color vision deficiency, the retina contains only rods and so the person cannot make any discriminations based on color. If lights of different wavelengths (colors) are adjusted to have the same luminance (brightness), a **rod monochromat** will not be able to distinguish between them. A monochromat can match any color (wavelength) with only one other color, so long as their luminances are adjusted appropriately. This type of deficiency can truly be called color blindness.

However, in the more common types of color vision deficiencies, people can perceive and distinguish a number of colors, confusing only a few. The most common type of color-deficient individual is the **dichromat**. A dichromat can match any color with a mixture of two other colors, in contrast to a normal **trichromat** who requires three colors to match any other. Dichromats are missing one of the three cone pigments that are present in individuals with normal color vision.

A person who is missing the green-sensitive (medium-wavelength sensitive) pigment is called a **deuteranope**, the most common type of color-deficient individual. A deuteranope is sensitive to, and can detect green light. However if the luminances are adjusted properly, they cannot tell the difference between green and red. A person who is missing the red-sensitive (long-wavelength sensitive) pigment is called a **protanope**. Although protanopes and deuteranopes both confuse red and green, the confusion is different in each of these deficiencies. A deuteranope has normal sensitivity to red light and is also relatively sensitive to the brightness of green light. A protanope on the other hand is very insensitive to red light. The result is that the two make color matches that are quite different and easy to identify with a color vision test. Another thing that protanopes and deuteranopes have in common is that both are dichormats, meaning they can match any color (wavelength) with a mixture of only two other colors. A third and very rare type of dichromat, the **tritanope**, is missing the blue-sensitive (short-wavelength sensitive) pigment.

In addition to dichromats who are missing one of the photopigments, there are people who have three pigments but still make what are considered abnormal color matches. These people are usually classified as **anomalous trichromats**. As with normal observers, anomalous trichromats require a mixture of three colors to match any other color, but the matches they make differ from those made by normal observers. For example, an anomalous trichromat may require more red than a normal observer to match yellow. He (most color-deficient people are men) would be classified as a **protanomalous trichromat**. This difference is caused by an abnormality in one of the pigments, rather than its total absence. A person that requires relatively more green in the mixture is classified as a **deuteranomalous trichromat**.

Color Mixing

Colors can be added together to create color mixtures in two different ways. When lights of different **wavelengths** are added together the process is called **additive color mixing**. When different colored paints (or inks, or pigments of any kinds) are mixed together it is called **subtractive color mixing**. The results of these two mixing processes are quite different. The artist must make very different assumptions about the mixing of paint than does the vision scientist about the mixing of light.

MIXING PIGMENTS (Subtractive Color Mixing)

When we apply paint to a surface, that paint affects the color of light that is reflected from that surface. When white light strikes paint, some of the light is absorbed by the pigments in the paint and some is reflected. For example, if white light strikes cyan-colored (bluish-green) paint, wavelengths corresponding to blue and green (the short wavelengths) are mostly reflected, and long wavelengths (yellow and red) are **mostly** absorbed. It is the reflected light that strikes the retinas in our eyes, causing us to see the color cyan. However, the reflected light contains other wavelengths as well—it is said to have a wide spectrum and may even contain a little red.

The same is true for paint that contains a yellow pigment. The wavelengths that are absorbed are mostly blue and the reflected light is made up of a wide spectrum that is mostly red and green. When red and green light in nearly equal amounts strike the retina, we see yellow.

When white light strikes a mixture of cyan and yellow paint, the wavelengths corresponding to red are absorbed by the cyan pigments in the paint, and the wavelengths corresponding to blue are absorbed by the yellow pigments. The left-over wavelengths that are reflected by both pigments are mostly green. We see green because the wavelengths corresponding to red and blue are **subtracted** from the white light and the remaining light that is reflected is mostly green. In other words, **when we look at a painted surface, we see the wavelengths of light that are reflected—the wavelengths of light that strike our retinas determine the colors we see.**

MIXING LIGHTS (Additive Color Mixing)

Mixing colored lights works in a very different way than mixing colored paints. We see color based on reflected light when we look at paint, but we see color based on emitted light when we look at lights. A light appears blue because it emits mostly wavelengths in the blue end of the spectrum. When blue light is mixed with yellow, the mixture contains both blue (short wavelengths) and yellow (medium and long wavelengths)—the two are added together—and the result is a neutral white or gray. In fact, yellow is the result of mixing red and green lights together. **The mixing of lights produces results that are the opposite of those produced by mixing paints—the result of adding versus subtracting wavelengths.** If colored lights from all parts of the visible spectrum are added together in equal amounts (or just the primary additive colors red, green, and blue) the result is white. If paints from all parts of the visible spectrum are added together in equal amounts the result is black.

Mach Bands

That apparent brightness is **not** a simple function of luminance has been known for some time now. It was Ernst Mach who, in 1865, first described what is now called a **Mach band** pattern. A Mach band is a region of enhanced contrast seen at the edges of neighboring regions that differ in brightness. In other words, when a lighter region is next to a darker region, the lighter region appears a little lighter and the darker region appears a little darker at the edge. Even though both regions are uniform in intensity, we see a region of enhanced contrast at the edge formed by the two regions. By enhancing contrast near edges, edges become more noticeable. This helps the visual system find edges and define the boundaries of objects in the world.

Mach bands are of interest because their existence suggests the presence of interactions between parts of the visual system that encode information about brightness in neighboring areas. These interactions are inhibitory and are called **lateral inhibition**. The process of lateral inhibition has been studied for a long time. The interactions responsible for lateral inhibition were first worked out in a series of experiments in the horseshoe crab *Limulus*. *Limulus* was used because it has a compound eye with large photoreceptors that make it easy to do this kind of research because the receptors could be stimulated individually.

The response of a photoreceptor is based not only on how much it is stimulated by light, but also by how much nearby photoreceptors are stimulated. In humans, photoreceptors can influence the response of their neighbors because they are connected to each other by horizontal and bipolar cells. These horizontal, or lateral, connections are mostly inhibitory and depend on photoreceptor stimulation. The higher the activity level of a photoreceptor, the greater the amount of inhibition produced. The effect of inhibition on other cells is also affected by distance—each cell is inhibited most by it closest neighbors. The result of this pattern of connections is that for any area of stimulation on the retina there is a center region of excitation surrounded by an area of inhibition. This type of response can be mathematically described by what is called a "Mexican hat" function (also known as a difference of Gaussians). Positive values in this function (above the horizontal axis) indicate excitation and negative values indicate inhibition; the greater the distance from the axis, the greater the amount of excitation or inhibition. Notice that the amount of inhibition is greatest near the center and gradually decreases with distance from the center.

How does this type of response profile produce contrast enhancement near luminance edges? In areas where the luminance of an object is uniform, neighboring areas of the retina produce a similar amount of excitation and inhibition, so neighboring cells have a similar response. However, at an edge (defined by a difference in luminance), the amount of excitation and inhibition produced by neighboring areas of the retina is not the same. On the side of the edge with the higher luminance both excitation and inhibition are relatively high. But on the side with the lower luminance both excitation and inhibition are relatively low.

Think about the response of a cell in the retina on the brighter side of the edge. Its excitation is high because it is stimulated by an area with high luminance. It receives inhibition from areas of high excitation on the brighter side and also from areas of lower excitation on the darker side. The result is that this cell on the brighter side of the edge is less inhibited than its neighbors on the brighter side, and its response is increased. Less inhibition means a larger response.

Now think about the response of a cell in the retina on the darker side of the edge. Its excitation is low because it is stimulated by an area with low luminance. It receives inhibition from areas of high excitation on the brighter side and also from areas of lower excitation on the darker side. The result is that this cell on the darker side of the edge is more inhibited than its neighbors on the darker side, and its response is decreased.

When you compare the responses of cells on both sides of the edge, you will see a region at the edge where the responses differ more than would be expected based on the difference in luminance alone. The perception produced by the responses of these cells is of an edge with enhanced contrast.

TO THE OWNER OF THIS BOOK:

I hope that you have found *InSight: A Media Lab in Experimental Psychology* useful. So that this book can be improved in a future edition, would you take the time to complete this sheet and return it? Thank you.

School and address: _____

_____

Department: _____

Instructor's name: _____

1. What I like most about this book is:_____

_____

_____

2. What I like least about this book is: _____

_____

_____

3. My general reaction to this book is: _____

_____

_____

4. The name of the course in which I used this book is: _____

_____

5. Were all of the chapters of the book assigned for you to read? _____

   If not, which ones weren't? _____

6. In the space below, or on a separate sheet of paper, please write specific suggestions for improving this book and anything else you'd care to share about your experience in using this book.

_____

_____

_____

_____

_____

_____

OPTIONAL:

Your name: _____ Date: _____

May we quote you, either in promotion for *InSight: A Media Lab in Experimental Psychology*,
or in future publishing ventures?

      Yes: _____ No: _____

      Sincerely yours,

      John A. Baro

ATTN: Marianne Taflinger

WADSWORTH/THOMSON LEARNING
10 DAVIS DRIVE
BELMONT, CA   94002-9801